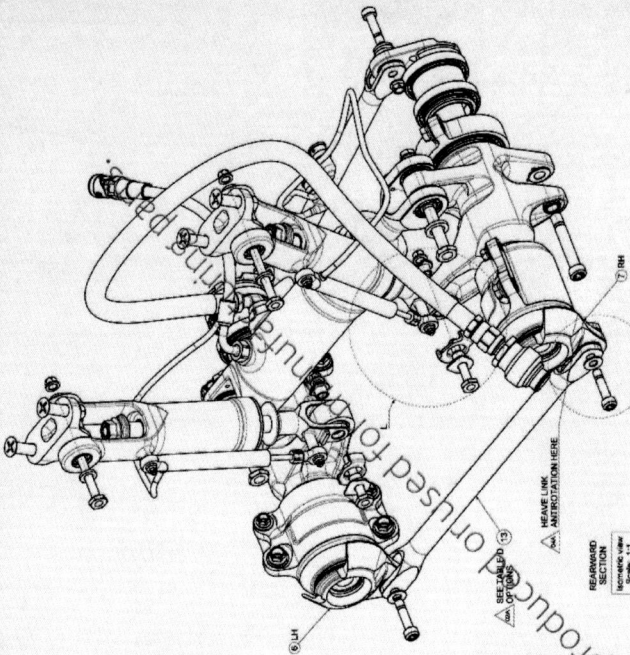

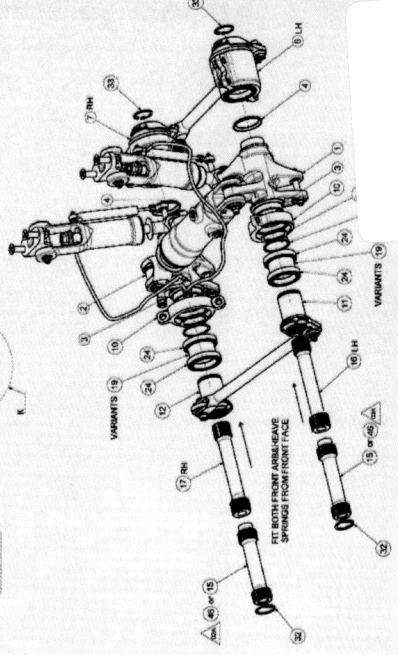

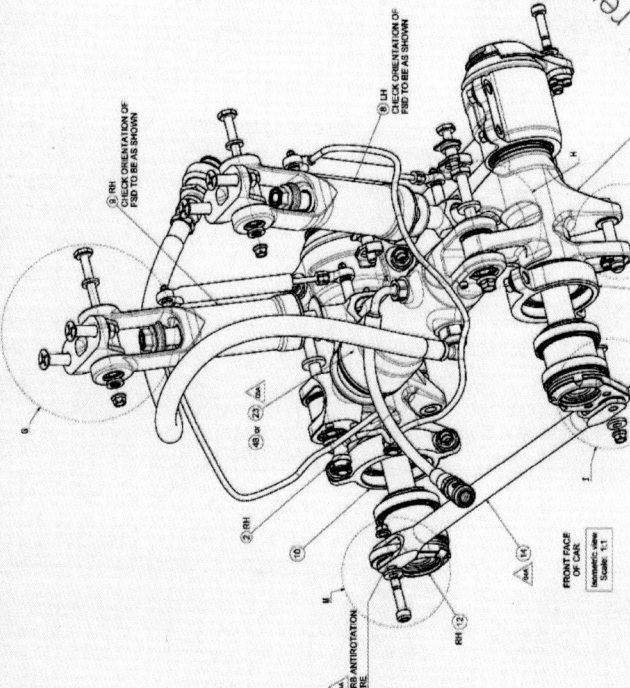

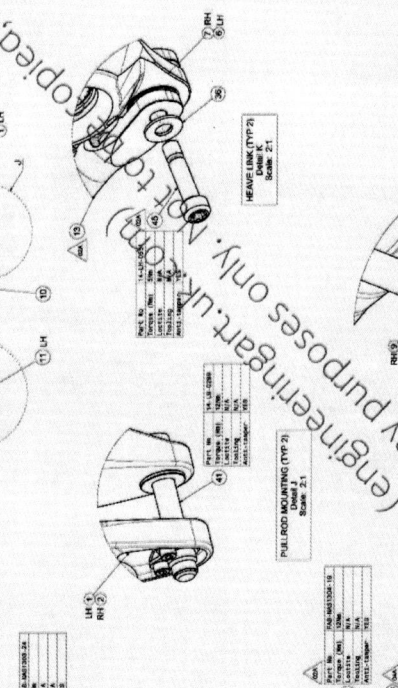

REARWARD SECTION
Isometric view
Scale: 1:1

FRONT FACE OF CAR
Isometric view
Scale: 1:1

HEAVE LINK (TYP 2)
Scale: 2:1

FSD TO ROCKER (TYP 2)
Detail L
Scale: 2:1

PULLROD MOUNTING (TYP 2)
Detail J
Scale: 2:1

HALS TO ROCKER (TYP 2)
Detail H
Scale: 1:1

FSD TOP MOUNT (TYP 2)
Detail G
Scale: 1:1

ARB LINK MOUNT LH
Detail I
Scale: 2:1

ARB LINK MOUNT RH
Detail M
Scale: 2:1

ASSEMBLY NOTES:

1. FIT FSD TOP BRKT (ITEMS 9) TO CHASSIS USING BOLTS (ITEMS 29)
   AND KNUT (ITEMS 31, 2 POSITIONS) (SEE DETAIL G).

2. PRESS FIT BEARINGS2 (ITEMS 33) AND SPACER (ITEM 19) TO FRONT
   CHASSIS BULKHEAD BRKTS (14-LB-0307/2) USING TOOL 14-LZ-0266.
   SECURE BEARINGS WITH LOCTITE 648 IF REQUIRED.
   DO NOT FIT FNH-H14-5 FOR FLVMB BRKT AS THIS STAGE. SEE SHEET 2.

3. PREASSEMBLE THRUST WASHERS (ITEMS 3 AND 4) TO ROCKER USING BOLT (ITEM 41). SEE DETAIL J
   AND THEN FIT ITEMS 6/7 AND 10 TO THEM.
   INSTALL TO STUDS IN CHASSIS SUPPORT BRKTS (14-LB-0054/0 AND 14-LB-0517B)
   USE FOR MODULES SPECIFIED. ASSEMBLE WITH CARE. SEE SHEET 2.
   APPLY TORQUES SPECIFIED.

4. ASSEMBLE THRUST WASHERS (ITEMS 3 AND 4) TO ARB ROCKERS (ITEMS 1&2)
   INSTALL ARB LINKWARDS ROCKERS TO FRONT BULKHEAD
   INSTALL ARB LINKWARDS ROCKERS TO FRONT BULKHEAD

5. ASSEMBLE ARB LINK (ITEM 14) TO ARB ROCKERS (ITEMS 1&2)
   TO THE CHASSIS, SEE DETAIL I AND M.
   SECURE WITH SHIM AND WASHER (ITEMS 34&42).

6. FIT FCA (ITEM 23048), SEE DETAIL H.

7. FIT FSD (ITEM 5/6) WITH ANTIROTATION TOP HATS TO ROCKER. SEE DETAIL.
   FIT FSD TO TOP CHASSIS BRKT (ITEM 5). SEE DETAIL G.
   CHECK ORIENTATION OF FSD IS AS SHOWN.

8. INSTALL HEAVE SPRINGS (ITEMS 15&6, 16/17) TO BE FITTED BOTH FROM CHASSIS
   FRONT FACE. SECURE WITH CIRCLIPS (32/33).

9. ARB AND HEAVE SPRINGS (ITEM 15/16, 16/17). CHECK TABLE D OPTIONS, SEE DETAIL K
   CHECK ORIENTATION OF FSD IS AS SHOWN.

TABLE A: TI ANTI-ROLL BAR 14-LH-0057 OPTIONS (ITEM 15)

TABLE B: STEEL ANTI-ROLL BAR 14-LH-0303 OPTIONS (ITEM 46)

TABLE C: HEAVE SPRING 14-LH-0305/A OPTIONS (ITEM 16/17)

TABLE D: HEAVE LINK V2 14-LH-0593 OPTIONS (ITEM 13)

Vehicle Dynamics

Andrew Greaney

About the Author

As a graduate from a Bachelors Honours Degree in Motorsport Technology and a successful graduate from a Foundation Engineering Degree in Motorsport Engineering has given me the knowledge to want to give something back to people who struggle to find the information and facts given within this book with a simple search engine. With a great amount of knowledge within this section of the motorsport, automotive and engineering industry, including the past five years of education and experiences, I do hope you gain knowledge and enjoy the short and sweet book. The aim of the book was to give the reader as much information as they would need without using confusing jargon or waffling around information of lesser importance.

With four years of experience working within the motorsport and engineering industry (at the time of publish), I have been through the thick and thin of what motorsport has to offer. The stressful, cold, wet, pressurised times to the successful, hot and cheerful days that the rewarding life of motorsport gives you. As a championship winning technician for a Formula Ford team I have experienced the rewards you get when you keep pushing. I have also engineered solutions for Mercedes AMG F1, Honda F1, the Aston Martin Valkyrie and many other race teams and high-performance cars while being an engineer of a world class exhaust fabrication company. I hope you enjoy this book and gain from it, as much as I did write it.

Contents

Table of Figures

1.0 Introduction

This study is researching into suspension design and layout on vehicles and how it affects them in the terms of roll centre control, camber and track change using relevant software. This includes reporting the different wishbone and axle layouts and designs, including location devices. These systems can include Watts, Panhard, Woblink, Mumford and others. The second section on this study is to report on the role of race car dampers. This is to discuss the types of dampers available, operation, testing methods, different forms of adjustability and how damping is decided for a given application. This also includes carrying out a test on a damper on a damper dynamometer, showing the process and analysis of the results.

This study relates to Motorsport by delving into performance vehicle suspension systems and dampers. Researching the suspension design and layout of these cars, and how they are affected while in motion. This will include the types of wishbones and axles used in these vehicles. Types of dampers used in Motorsport vehicles will be covered along with the operation and adjustability of the explained dampers. The testing on dampers on a dynamometer to visually see how the damper performs on a graph at different speeds.

The second section of the study is delving into the dynamics and suspension systems of a single seater performance car. This will be looking at the set-up sheets, geometry, corner weights, suspension systems and other related dynamics of a single seater performance car. A practical task must be performed where the current settings of the single seater performance car will be recorded and analysed. Required adjustments will be carried out if needed in order to get the vehicle into the correct set up. This will be shown with evidence in how they were carried out, along with what difference does this make to the driving dynamics of the vehicle. An inspection of this vehicle will be made critiquing its readiness to race. This will be carried out on the vehicle's suspension, tyres, wheels and steering showing their suitability to race and resolving any problems that occur. Then the single seater performance car will be analysed to show why it is a competitive racing vehicle. Handling characteristics, suspension type, steering and tyres will be analysed to show the effect on handling and stability of the vehicle.

The second section of the study is a discussion on the advantages and disadvantages of different suspension systems which are used on competition vehicles. These include double wishbone suspension, rocker arm, MacPherson strut and pushrod to name a few.

This second section relates to Motorsport by relating to single seater performance cars and how they are set up, suspension and geometry wise. By understand how the suspension systems work together along with the geometry changes to show why that makes the vehicle faster around a track. Creating set up sheets are useful and quick ways to know what to do and set up on a vehicle.

The third section of the study looks into basics of vehicle dynamics including the sections below:

- Basics
- Wheels and Tyres
- Chassis
- Weight
- Vehicle Adjustment
- Suspension
- Weight Distribution
- Polar Moment of Inertia
- Suspension Development – regarding double wishbone suspension
- Anti-Roll Bars
- King Pin Inclination (KPI)
- Steering Axis Inclination (SAI)
- Scrub Angle
- Rear Suspension
- Motion Ratio and Wheel Rates
- Springs
- Car Set Up and Handling Issues
- Steering
- Ackermann

And many subsections within these topics.

2.0 Suspension Design

This first section creates a study, using relevant software, to show how suspension design and layout affects a cars performance in terms of Roll Centre control, camber and track change. Including studies of various wishbone and axle layouts (including locations devices – Watts, Woblink, Panhard, Mumford, etc).

Double wishbone suspension is among the most common suspension designs used on performance vehicles. This is due to a double wishbone layout causing less drag, as inboard designs allow the damper to not be in the freestream. The design offers a "greater steering response as steering axis is spate to the vertical motion" (Balancemotorsport.co.uk, 2016). Roll centre can also be controlled "within a limited range of motion" (Balancemotorsport.co.uk, 2016), giving a more consistent location of roll centre. The roll centre is a geometric joint which cannot be seen, as shown in Figure 1. The roll centre is the point of which a given axle rotates around (the sprung mass). There is a roll centre at the front and rear of every vehicle. Double wishbone suspension also allows for a large range of adjustability and freedom of design.

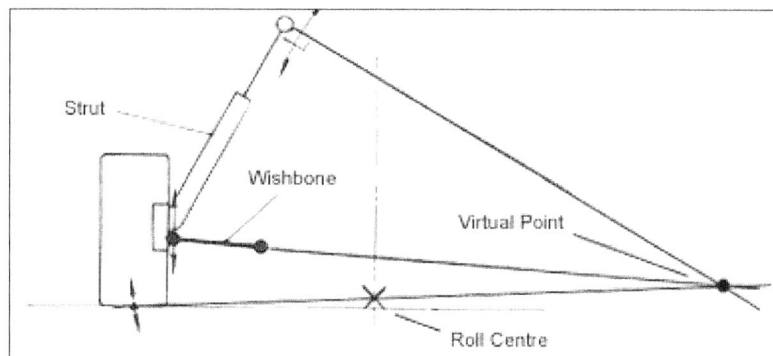

Figure 1 - Roll Centre

(Suspension Geometry, 2016)

The virtual point is also known as the instantaneous centre (IC). The roll couple (also known as the roll moment) is the relationship between the centre of gravity and roll centre at a given axle. The roll centre can be used as a fine-tuning device. Usually the rear roll centre is higher than the front. The relationship between front and rear through the axis must remain as stable as possible. The closer the roll couple, the less weight transfer occurs due to leverage forces. Lower front roll centre offers:

- More on throttle steering
- Better on smooth, high grip tracks with long fast corners
- Less responsive car due to the larger roll couple
- Rear will have less roll giving it a tendency to slide

A higher front roll centre offers:

- More responsive car
- Less on throttle steering
- Use on tracks with quick direction changes (chicanes)
- Use in high grip conditions to avoid traction rolling

A lower rear roll centre offers:

- Increased traction (at the cost of tyre wear)
- Use under low traction conditions
- Use to avoid traction rolling at corner entry (increases the rear grip)
- More on throttle grip
- Less grip under braking
- More chassis roll due to the weight transfer onto the outside wheel
- Less traction under braking due to more weight transfer onto the front

A higher rear roll centre offers:

- More responsive car
- Less on throttle steering
- Use on tracks with quick direction changes (chicanes)
- Use in high grip conditions to avoid traction rolling

It is usually seen that the front roll centre is $\frac{2}{3}$ of the rear roll centre height. The lower roll centre gives more roll angle which is controlled with the anti-roll bar.

Double wishbone layouts consist of:

- Equal and parallel

- Equal and non-parallel
- Non-equal and non-parallel

(Roll Center Understood, 2016)

The different layout of double wishbone suspension can range from parallel to un-parallel and/or equal and un-equal, each one offering different characteristics, such as camber, track changes and "wheel control during dynamic travel" (Smith, 2013). With equal and parallel double wishbone suspension the roll centre is located on the ground, this means that there is no camber change while bump or rebound is occurring. Although there is track change while bump or rebound occurs. "The outside wheel changes towards positive camber during chassis roll by the same angle as the chassis roll" (Smith, 2013). Camber and track change can be reduced by using longer wishbones, although it is not removed complete.

On unequal and parallel the upper wishbone is usually the shorter wishbone. This creates negative camber on the wheel, which increases while bump occurs and while rebound occurs the camber can change to positive or negative. The amount of track change is negligible. When roll occurs "the outside wheel will lose a small amount of negative camber, while the inside wheel tends to gain more negative camber" (Smith, 2013). The location of the roll centre is stable (around ground level), this allows for a good roll couple.

With unequal and un-parallel, the roll centre is placed anywhere while the suspension is stationary. Wishbones that incline into the chassis provides a better control of camber change in roll. Track change is negligible and there is "more freedom of camber curves in vertical movement and roll" (Smith, 2013).

A piece of software was used to analyse each one of these layouts in different circumstances. These circumstances are roll centre, camber changes and track change during bump, rebound, roll and an un-flat floor.

The first simulation was on equal and parallel wishbones. The first table shows this carried out without any bump, rebound or roll (in a resting state). This shows the ride height being 170 mm with the roll centre being -23 mm underneath the ground.

	Equal & Parallel Resting	
	L	R
Ride Height = 170 mm		
Roll Centre = -23 mm		
Camber	-2.7°	-2.7°
Horizontal Change	0 mm	0 mm
Vertical Change	0 mm	0 mm
Instant Roll Centre	-559260 mm:19700 mm	559260 mm:19700 mm

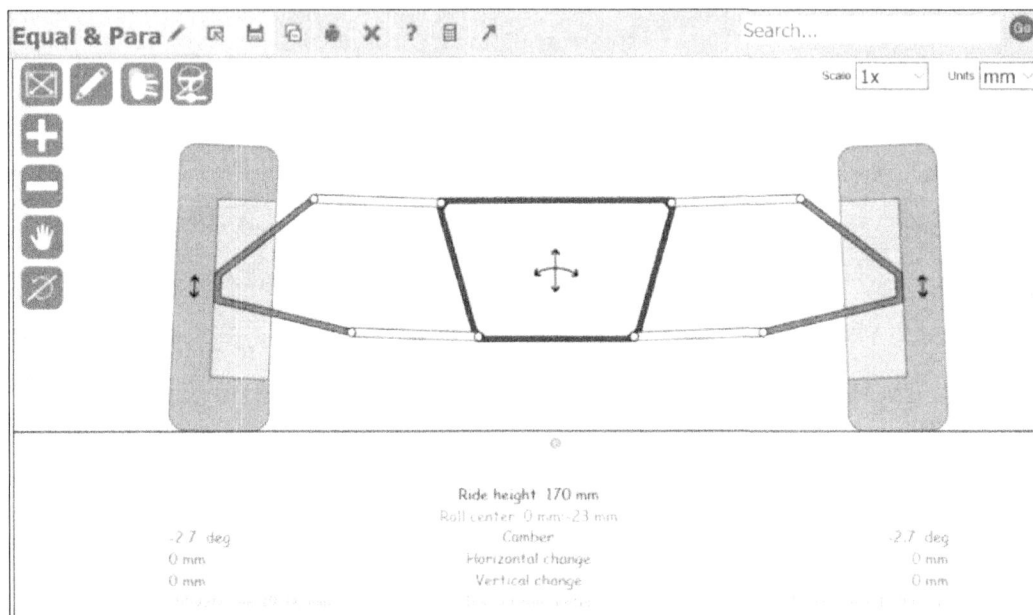

Figure 2 - Equal & Parallel Wishbones Resting

	Equal & Parallel Bump	
	L	R
Ride Height = 160 mm		
Roll Centre = -49 mm		
Camber	-2.7°	-2.7°
Horizontal Change	-1 mm	-1 mm
Vertical Change	0 mm	0 mm
Instant Roll Centre	-562822 mm:43132 mm	562822 mm:43132 mm

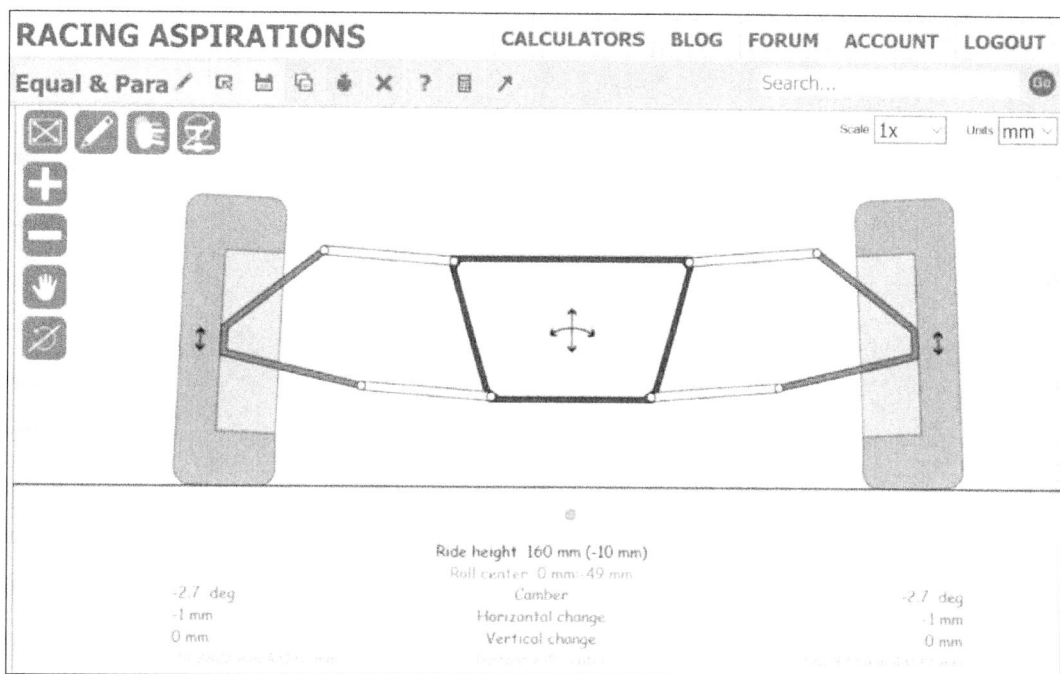

Figure 3 - Equal & Parallel Wishbones Bump

	Equal & Parallel Rebound	
	L	R
Ride Height = 180 mm		
Roll Centre = 4 mm		
Camber	-2.7°	-2.7°
Horizontal Change	0 mm	0 mm
Vertical Change	0 mm	0 mm
Instant Roll Centre	-553129 mm:-3450 mm	553129 mm:-3450 mm

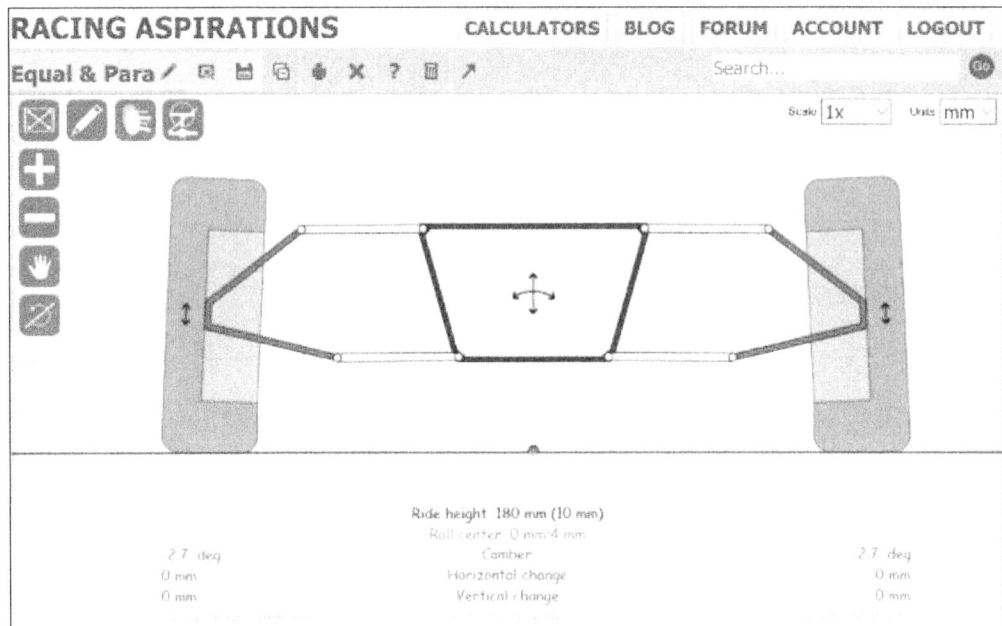

Figure 4 - Equal & Parallel Wishbones Rebound

	Equal & Parallel Roll (Left)	
	L	R
Chassis Roll	5°	-5°
Ride Height = 172 mm		
Roll Centre = 3488 mm:-493 mm		
Camber	2.5°	7.7°
Horizontal Change	-19 mm	11 mm
Vertical Change	0 mm	0 mm
Instant Roll Centre	-564218 mm:67647 mm	478886 mm:-83215 mm

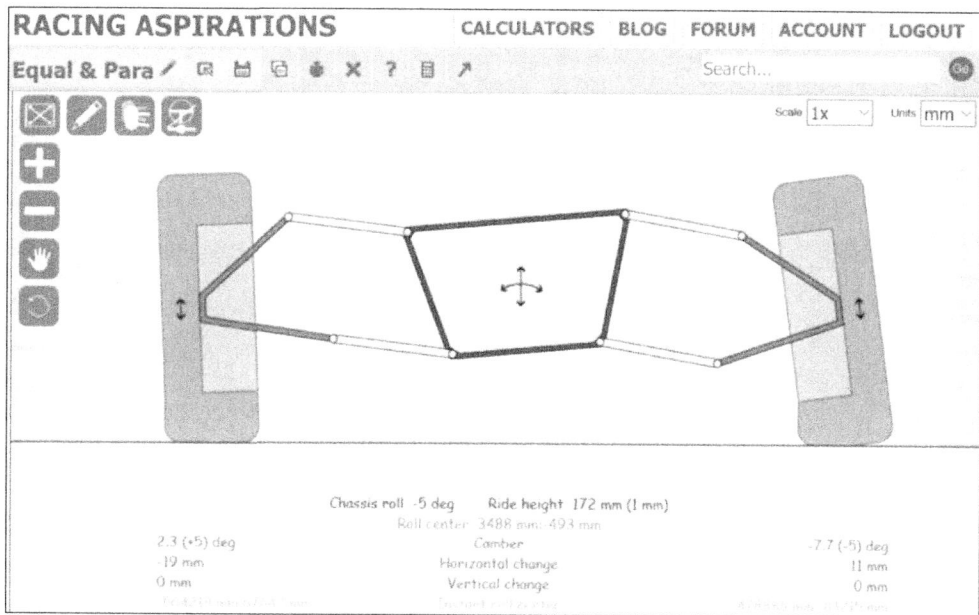

Figure 5 - Equal & Parallel Wishbones Roll Left

	Equal & Parallel Roll (Right)	
	L	**R**
Chassis Roll	-5°	5°
Ride Height = 172 mm		
Roll Centre = -3488 mm:-493 mm		
Camber	-7.7°	2.3°
Horizontal Change	11 mm	-19 mm
Vertical Change	0 mm	0 mm
Instant Roll Centre	-478886 mm:-83215 mm	564218 mm:67647 mm

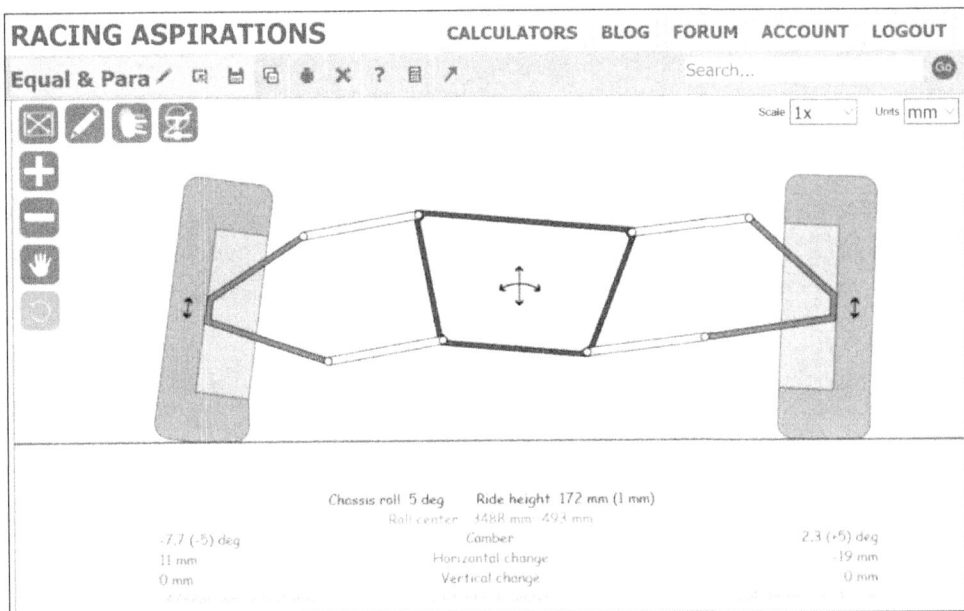

Figure 6 - Equal & Parallel Wishbones Roll Right

	Equal & Parallel Right Bump	
	L	R
Ride Height = 151 mm		
Roll Centre = 264 mm:-55 mm		
Camber	-2.7°	-2.7°
Horizontal Change	0 mm	-3 mm
Vertical Change	0 mm	32 mm
Instant Roll Centre	-559260 mm:33614 mm	560996 mm:81618 mm

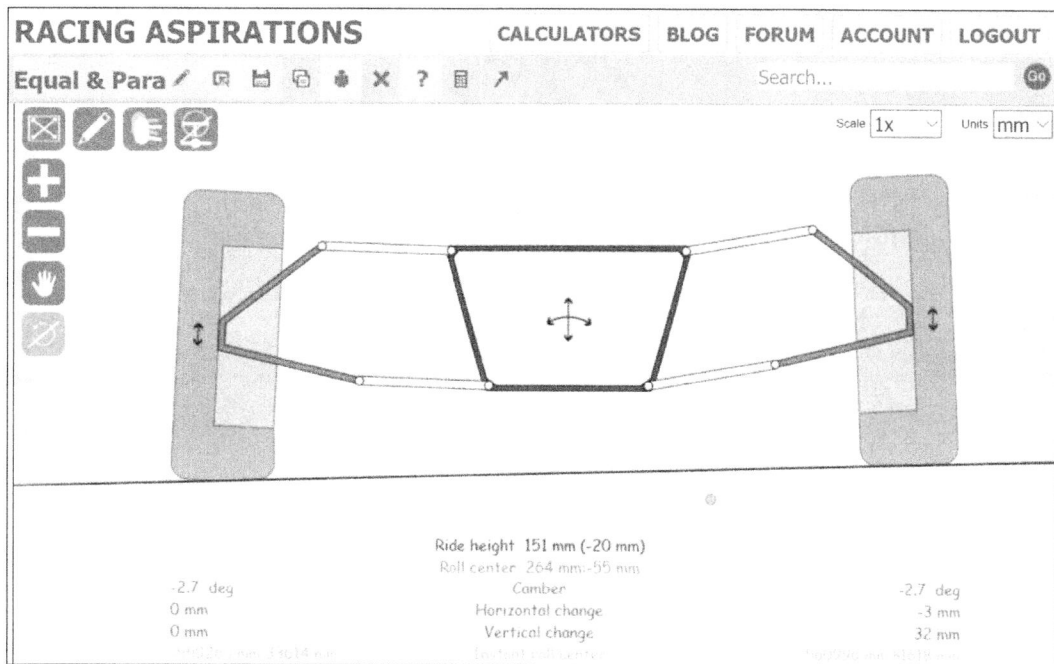

Figure 7 - Equal & Parallel Wishbones Un-flat Floor Right

	Equal & Parallel Bump (Left)	
	L	**R**
Ride Height = 190 mm		
Roll Centre = 592 mm:7 mm		
Camber	-2.7°	-2.7°
Horizontal Change	0 mm	-4 mm
Vertical Change	0 mm	-52 mm
Instant Roll Centre	-559260 mm:-2979 mm	502262 mm:-72107 mm

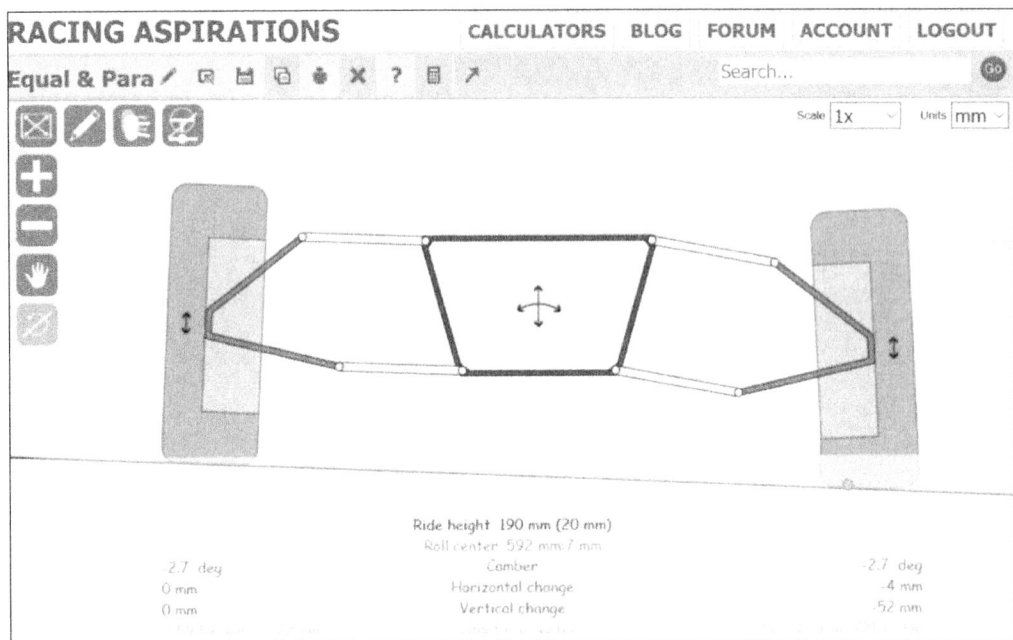

Figure 8 - Equal & Parallel Wishbones Un-flat Floor Left

	Un-Equal & Parallel Resting	
	L	R
Ride Height = 163 mm		
Roll Centre = 0 mm:-23 mm		
Camber	-2.7°	-2.7°
Horizontal Change	0 mm	0 mm
Vertical Change	0 mm	0 mm
Instant Roll Centre	-559260 mm:19692 mm	559260 mm:19692 mm

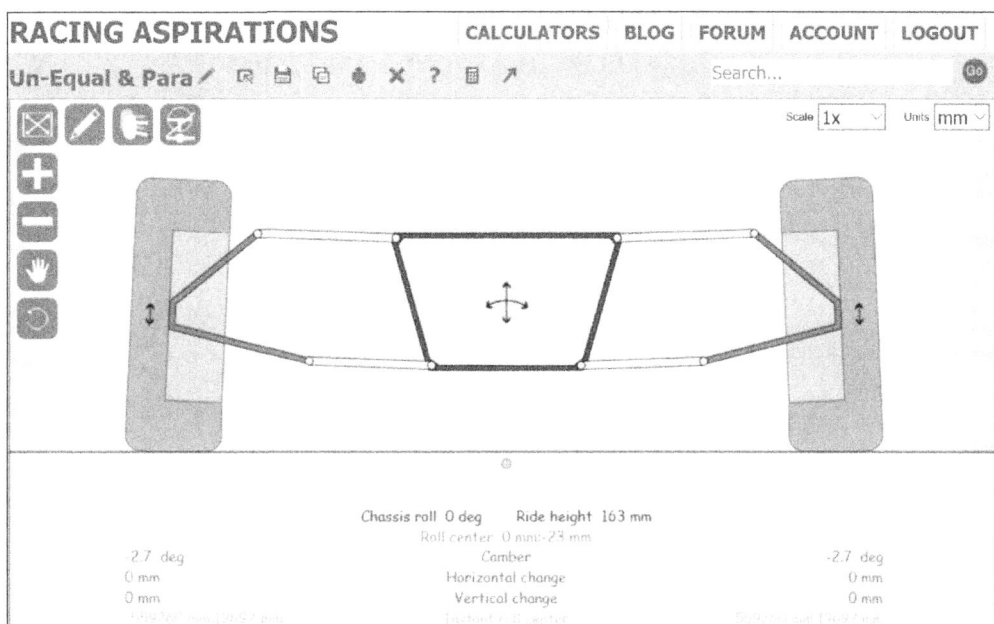

Figure 9 - Un-Equal & Parallel Wishbones Resting

	Un-Equal & Parallel Bump	
	L	R
Ride Height = 153 mm		
Roll Centre = 0 mm:-53 mm		
Camber	-2.7°	-2.7°
Horizontal Change	-1 mm	-1 mm
Vertical Change	0 mm	0 mm
Instant Roll Centre	-47468 mm:3780 mm	47468 mm:3780 mm

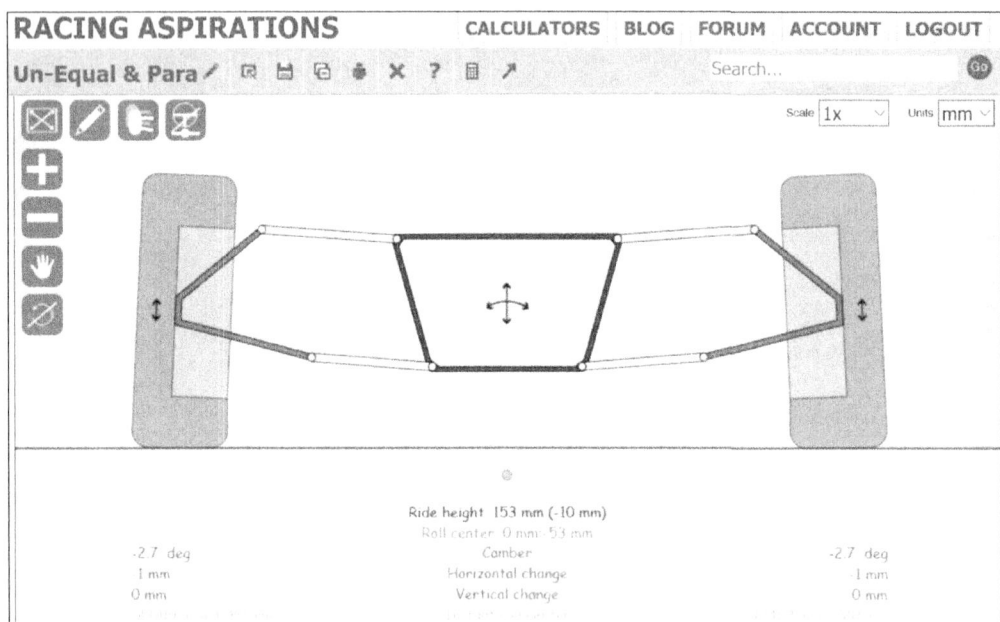

Figure 10 - Un-Equal & Parallel Wishbones Bump

	Un-Equal & Parallel Rebound	
	L	**R**
Ride Height = 153 mm		
Roll Centre = 0 mm:-53 mm		
Camber	-2.7°	-2.7°
Horizontal Change	-1 mm	-1 mm
Vertical Change	0 mm	0 mm
Instant Roll Centre	-47468 mm:3780 mm	47468 mm:3780 mm

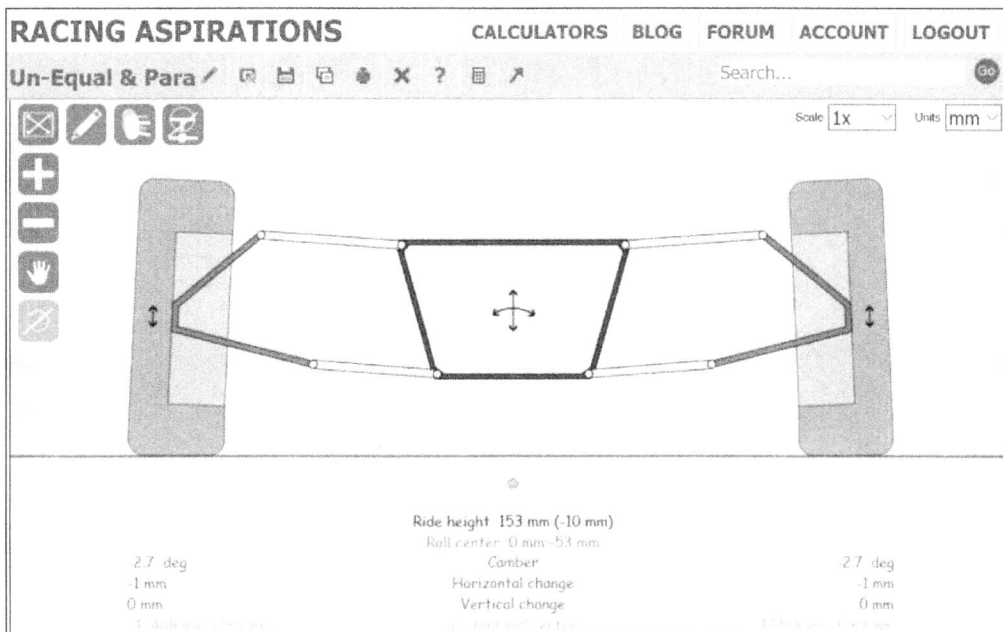

Figure 11 - Un-Equal & Parallel Wishbones Rebound

	Un-Equal & Parallel Roll (Left)	
	L	**R**
Chassis Roll	5.1°	-4.7°
Ride Height = 164 mm		
Roll Centre = 5931 mm:-976 mm		
Camber	2.4°	-7.4°
Horizontal Change	-19 mm	10 mm
Vertical Change	0 mm	0 mm
Instant Roll Centre	-10922 mm:1529 mm	-7977 mm:1601 mm

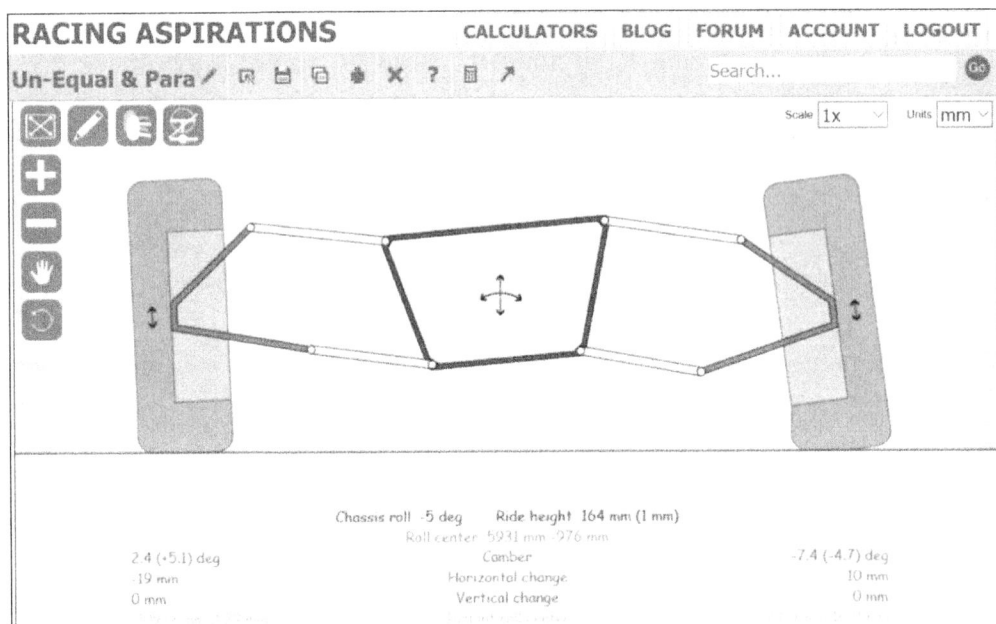

Figure 12 - Un-Equal & Parallel Wishbones Roll Left

	Un-Equal & Parallel Roll (Right)	
	L	R
Chassis Roll	-4.7°	5.1°
Ride Height = 164 mm		
Roll Centre = -5931 mm:-976 mm		
Camber	-7.4°	2.4°
Horizontal Change	10 mm	-19 mm
Vertical Change	0 mm	0 mm
Instant Roll Centre	7977 mm:1601 mm	10922 mm:1529 mm

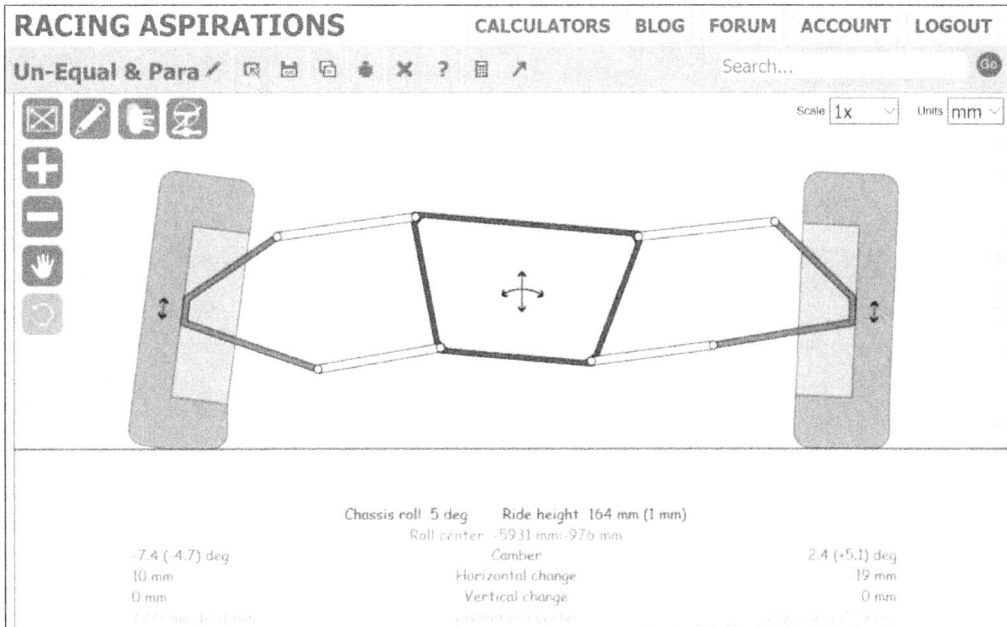

Figure 13 - Un-Equal & Parallel Wishbones Roll Right

	Un-Equal & Parallel Bump (Right)	
	L	**R**
Ride Height = 143 mm		
Roll Centre = 300 mm:-57 mm		
Camber	-2.7°	-2.6°
Horizontal Change	0 mm	-4 mm
Vertical Change	0 mm	32 mm
Instant Roll Centre	-559260 mm:33385 mm	14560 mm:2269 mm

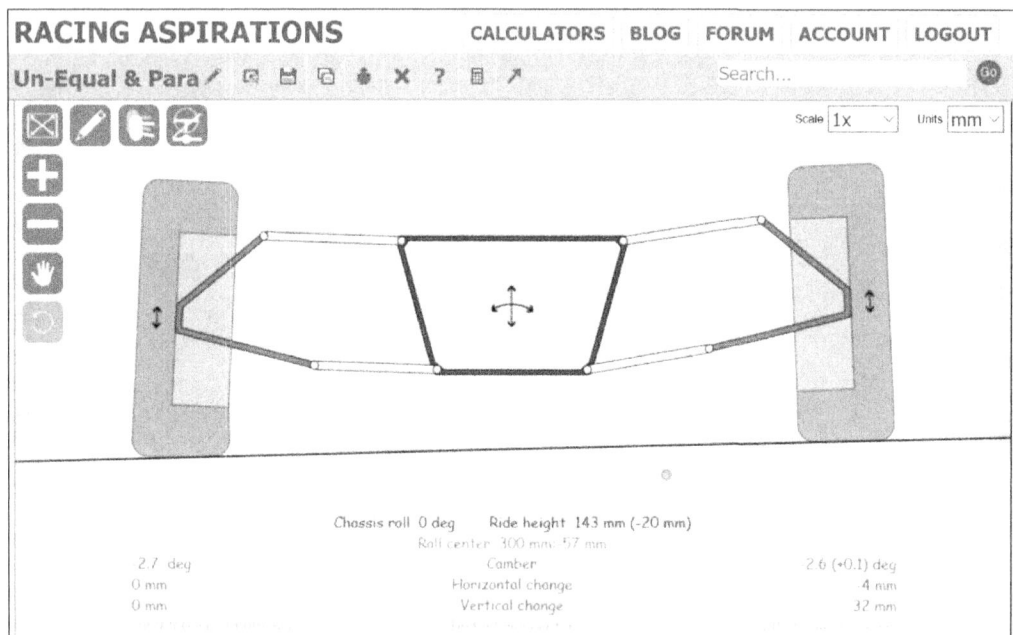

Figure 14 - Un-Equal & Parallel Wishbones Un-flat Floor Right

	Un-Equal & Parallel Bump (Left)	
	L	R
Ride Height = 183 mm		
Roll Centre = 611 mm:6 mm		
Camber	-2.7°	-2.6°
Horizontal Change	0 mm	-4 mm
Vertical Change	0 mm	52 mm
Instant Roll Centre	-559260 mm:-2578 mm	-10877 mm:1764 mm

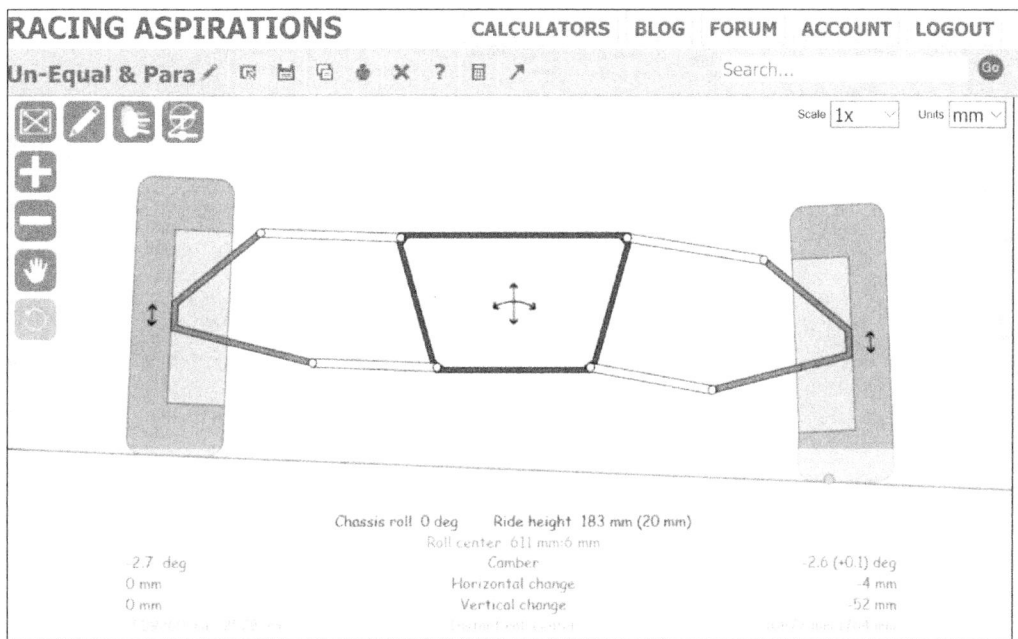

Figure 15 - Un-Equal & Parallel Wishbones Un-flat Floor Left

	Un-Equal & Un-Parallel Resting	
	L	**R**
Ride Height = 154 mm		
Roll Centre = 0mm:-7mm		
Camber	-2.7°	-2.7°
Horizontal Change	0 mm	0 mm
Vertical Change	0 mm	0 mm
Instant Roll Centre	6760 mm:-82 mm	-6760 mm:-82 mm

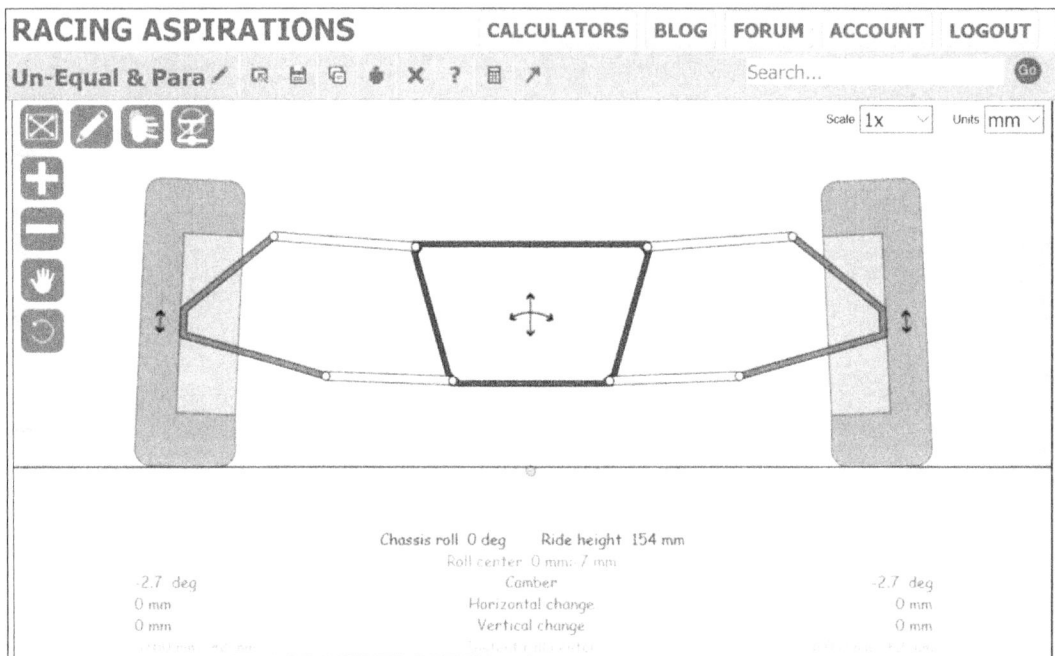

Figure 16 - Un-Equal & Un-Parallel Wishbones Resting

	Un-Equal & Un-Parallel Bump	
	L	R
Ride Height = 144 mm		
Roll Centre = 0 mm:-34 mm		
Camber	-2.8°	-2.8
Horizontal Change	0 mm	0 mm
Vertical Change	0 mm	0 mm
Instant Roll Centre	7504 mm:-427 mm	-7504 mm:-427 mm

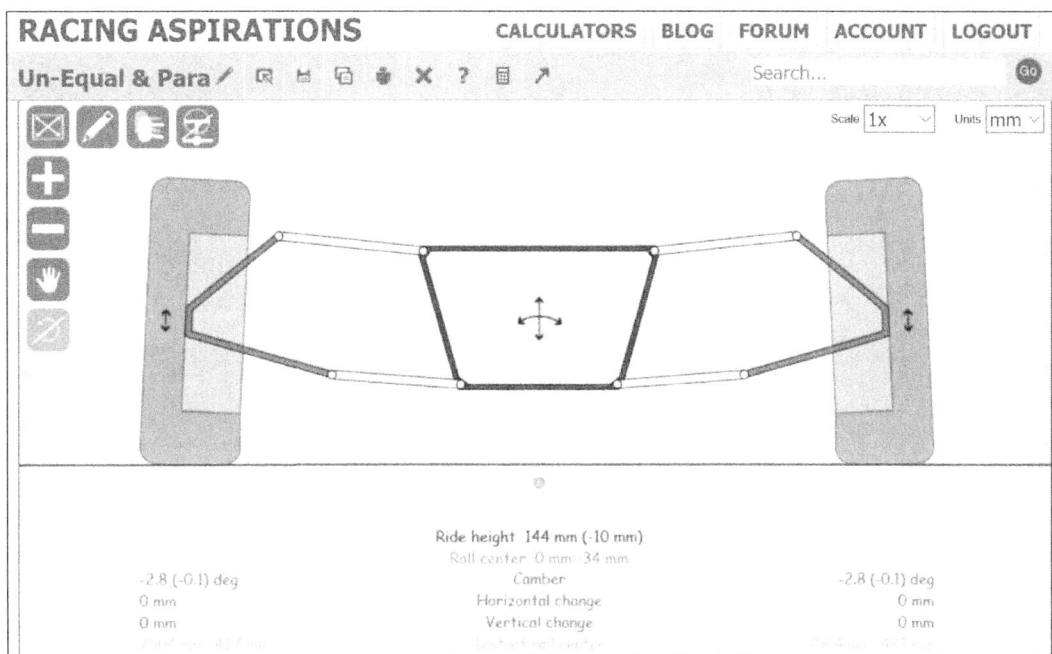

Figure 17 - Un-Equal & Un-Parallel Wishbones Bump

	Un-Equal & Un-Parallel Rebound	
	L	R
Ride Height = 164 mm		
Roll Centre = 0 mm:19mm		
Camber	-2.6°	-2.6°
Horizontal Change	0 mm	0 mm
Vertical Change	0 mm	0 mm
Instant Roll Centre	6159 mm:198 mm	-6159 mm:198 mm

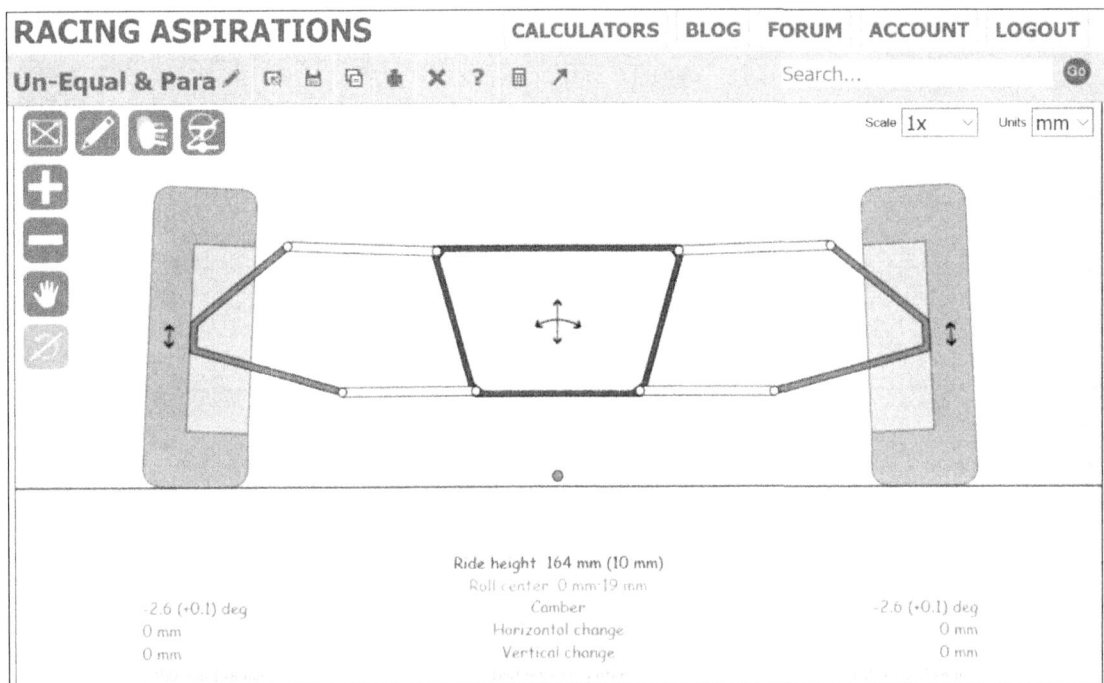

Figure 18 - Un-Equal & Un-Parallel Wishbones Rebound

	Un-Equal & Un-Parallel Roll (Left)	
	L	R
Chassis Roll	5.1°	-4.7°
Ride Height = 164 mm		
Roll Centre = 5931 mm:-976 mm		
Camber	2.4°	-7.4°
Horizontal Change	-19 mm	10 mm
Vertical Change	0 mm	0 mm
Instant Roll Centre	-10922 mm:1529 mm	-7977 mm:1601 mm

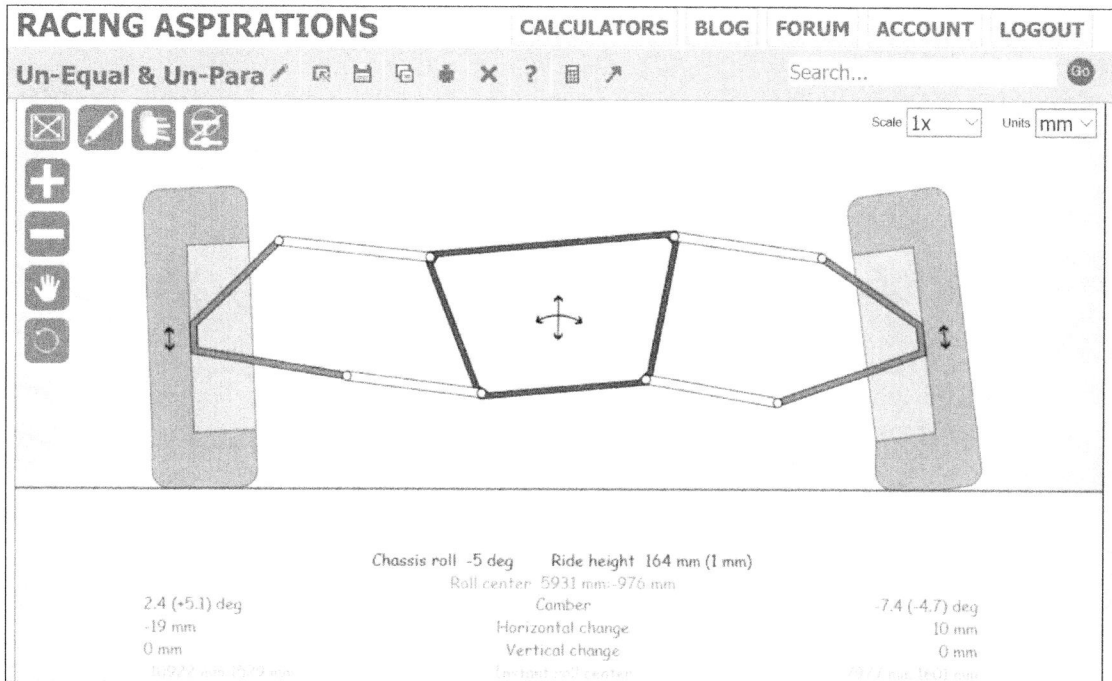

Figure 19 - Un-Equal & Un-Parallel Wishbones Roll Left

	Un-Equal & Un-Parallel Roll (Right)	
	L	R
Chassis Roll	-4.7°	5.1
Ride Height = 164 mm		
Roll Centre = -5931 mm:-976 mm		
Camber	-7.4°	2.4°
Horizontal Change	10 mm	-19 mm
Vertical Change	0 mm	0 mm
Instant Roll Centre	7977 mm:1601 mm	10922 mm:1529 mm

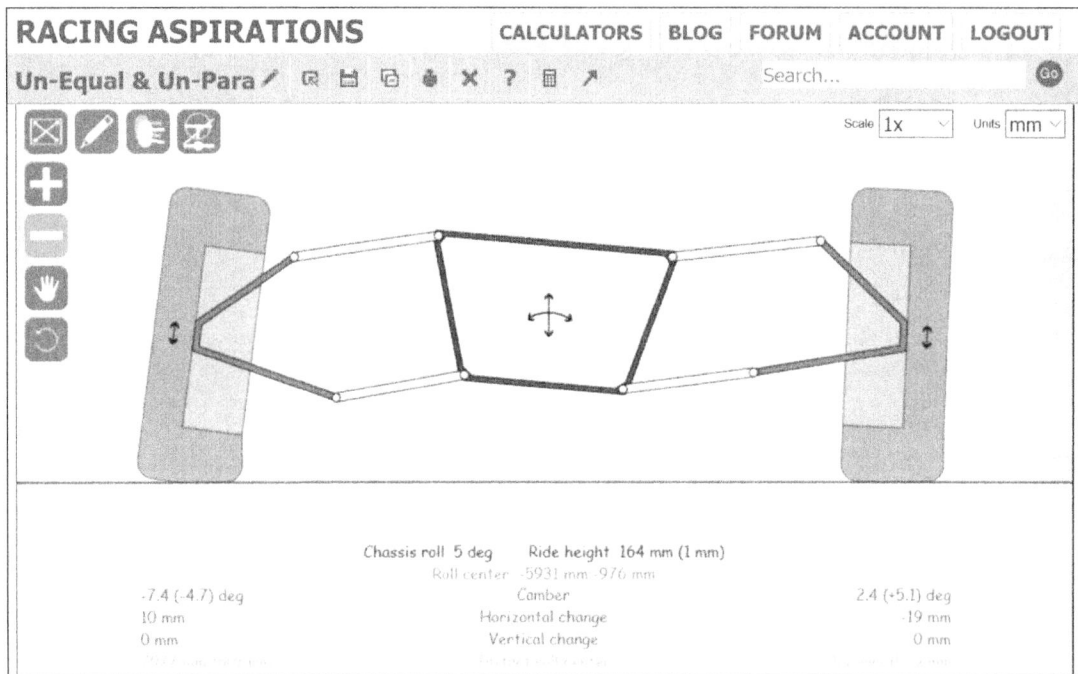

Figure 20 - Un-Equal & Un-Parallel Wishbones Roll Right

	Un-Equal & Un-Parallel Bump (Right)	
	L	R
Ride Height = 143 mm		
Roll Centre = 300 mm:-57 mm		
Camber	-2.7°	-2.6°
Horizontal Change	0 mm	-4 mm
Vertical Change	0 mm	32 mm
Instant Roll Centre	-559260 mm:33385 mm	14560 mm:2269 mm

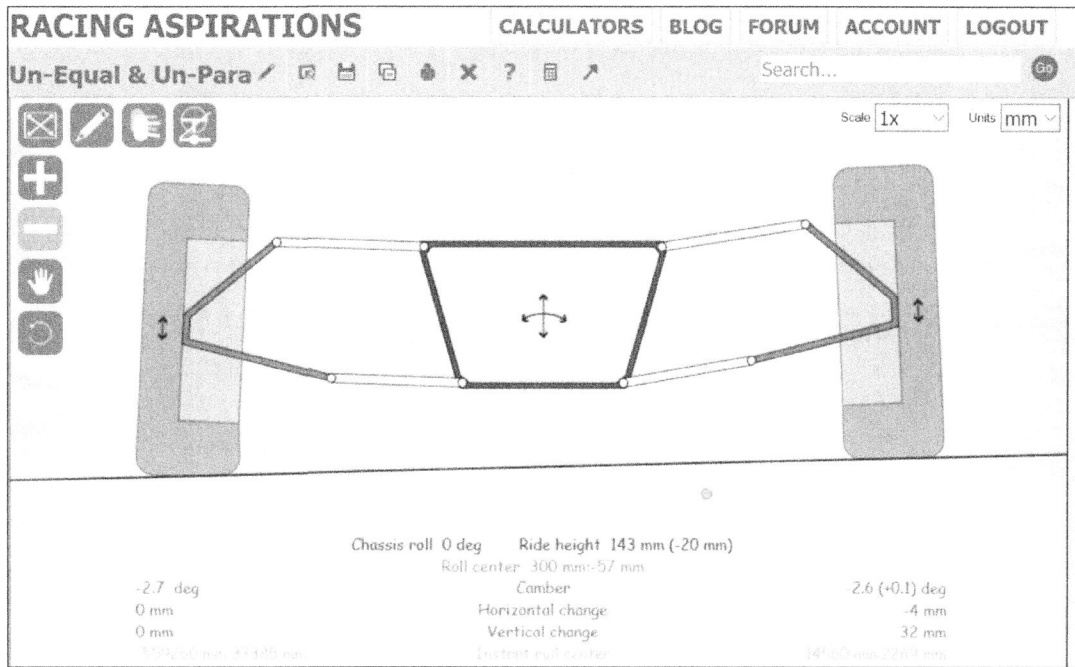

Figure 21 - Un-Equal & Un-Parallel Wishbones Un-flat Floor Right

	Equal & Parallel Bump (Left)	
	L	R
Ride Height = 183 mm		
Roll Centre = 611 mm:6 mm		
Camber	-2.7°	-2.6°
Horizontal Change	0 mm	-4 mm
Vertical Change	0 mm	-52 mm
Instant Roll Centre	-559260 mm:-2578 mm	-10877 mm:1764 mm

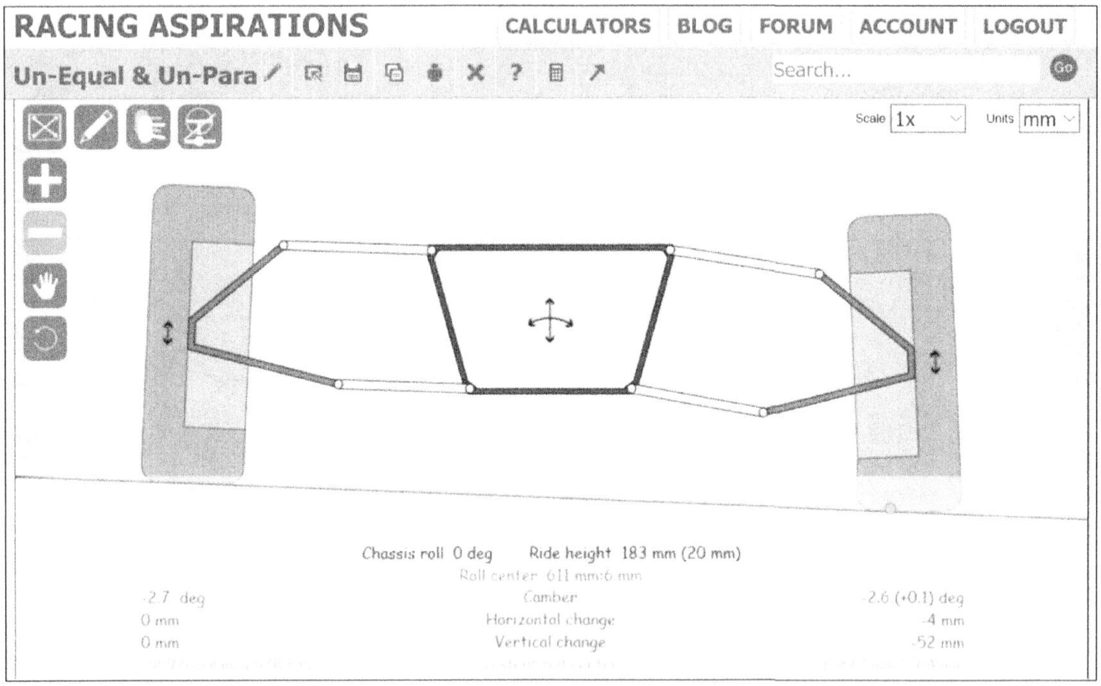

Figure 22 - Un-Equal & Un-Parallel Wishbones Un-flat Floor Left

Each one of these double wishbone designs have their advantages and disadvantages, but the best layout would be unequal and un-parallel due to providing more camber gain, keeping more of the tyre in contact with the ground (very important for race cars) during bump situations.

A rear live axle is a rear axle that has drive going through it, this can be seen in rear wheel drive cars. An example is shown in Figure 23. A dead rear axle is a rear axle without drive going through it, this can be seen on front wheel drive cars. Advantages to this system is that it is cheap to produce, can handle higher torque, have less losses due to independent designs have more universal joints and more angles. Disadvantages to a live axle is that both wheels are connected and not individually sprung, so an effect on one wheel has an effect on the other, which could unbalance the car, or cause to loose traction on both tyres. This system also has a higher unsprung weight and that there is limited adjustability due to the wheels being attached to the axle. (Boards.straightdope.com, 2016). De-Dion suspension is a similar design to this.

Figure 23 also shows an example on a Panhard suspension system. it stops the rear axle from moving sideways. This makes handling predictable "and it also allows for tuning of the rear roll centre" (Timskelton.com, 2016). Advantages of this system is that it is light weight and not extremely complex. Disadvantages include a higher unsprung weight, opposing side contact patch is affected and it has limited adjustability.

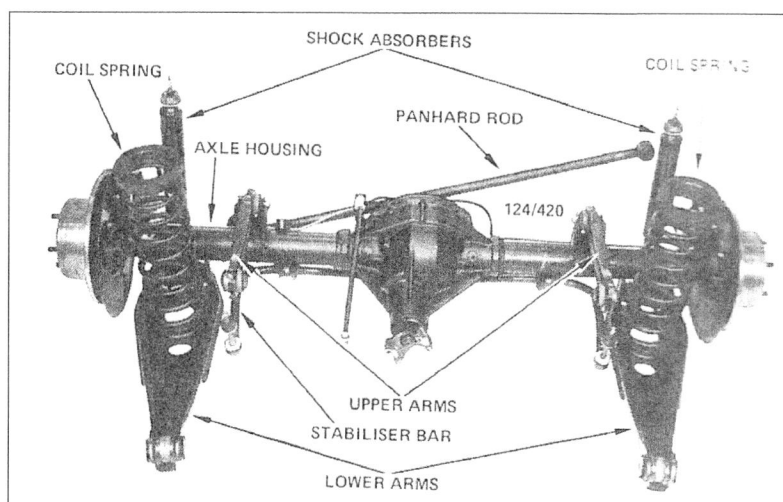

Figure 23 - Live Axle

(Forums.justcommodores.com.au, 2011)

Watts linkage (Figure 24) is a pivot on the differential which is connected by links that mount on the chassis. This means rebound, bump and roll are controlled. Advantages of this suspension is the low weight and non-complex. Disadvantages include a higher unsprung weight, opposing side contact patch is affected and it has limited adjustability.

Advantages of Mumford (Figure 25) and Woblink (Figure 26) suspension is the low weight and non-complex. Disadvantages include a higher unsprung weight, opposing side contact patch is affected and it has limited adjustability, similar to the other designs.

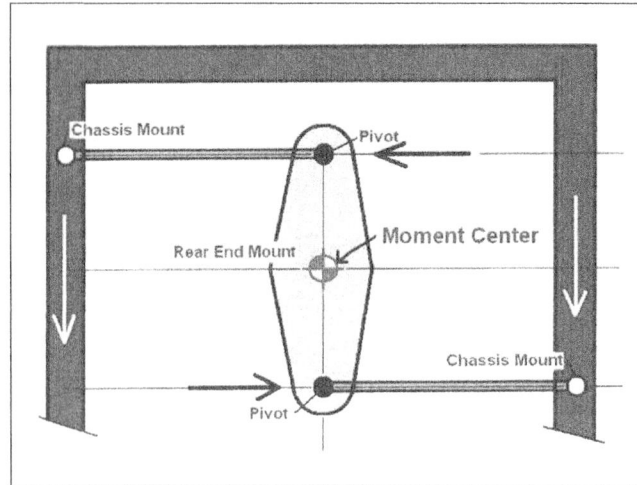

Figure 24 - Watts Linkage

(Bolles, 2008)

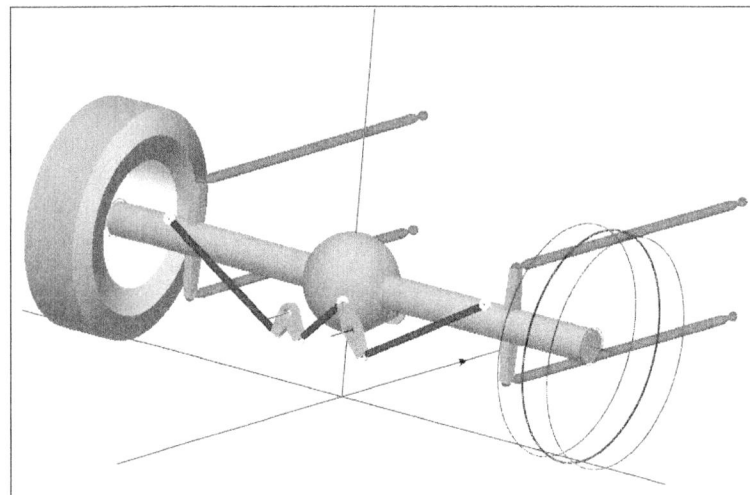

Figure 25 - Mumford Suspension

(Susprog.com, 2016)

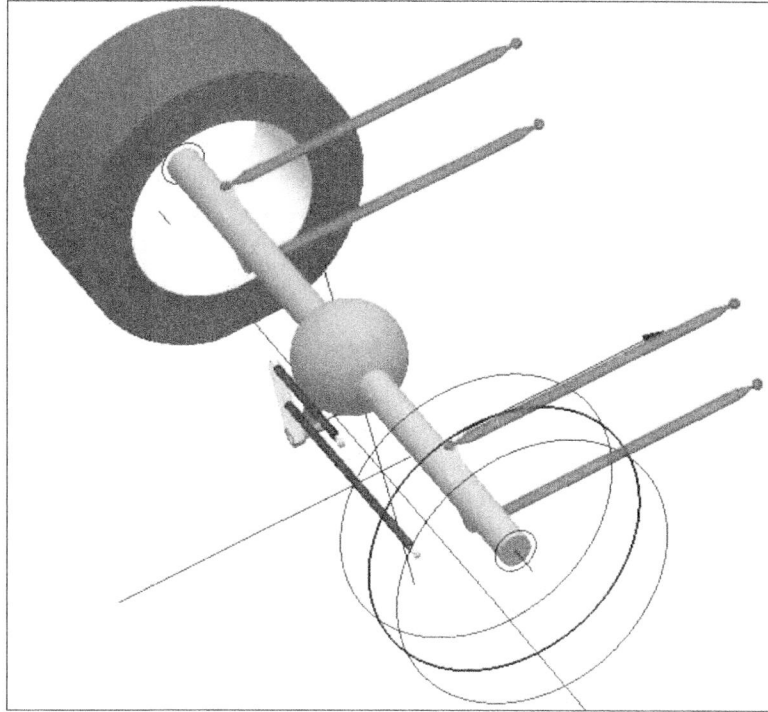

Figure 26 - Woblink Suspension

(Young, 2016)

3.0 Dampers

This second section of the study will be reporting on the role of race car dampers. This will discuss the types available (including Inerter), operation, adjustability, testing methods and how damping is decided for a given application. Including a test on a damper using a dynamometer, detailing the process and analysing the results gained

Dampers are used to dampen out the spring's movement, controlling how the suspension moves. "The damper acts as a grip adjustment tool and can also have an impact of tyre degradation" (Smith, 2013). The damper is designed to convert the kinetic energy created from the spring and turn it into heat energy which is absorbed by the oil in the damper. Dampers can also be used for tuning and adjusting (useful for corner weighting and geometry). Dampers work by using a piston inside within oil chambers, which move up and down with the suspension. The oil is forced through holes, in which the size of decides how soft or hard the damper is and how quick the damper moves. There is valving located in this piston which has "calibrated shims that deflect at certain forces, and it is this deflection that allows the oil to pass through" (Smith, 2013). Most dampers are adjusted using C-spanners for the preload and ride height, located at the bottom of the damper (Figure 27).

Figure 27 - Preload Adjustment on a Damper

There are many different variants of dampers such as closed and open lengths, construction, materials, mounting, shaft sizing, eyelets and adjustment. The range of adjustment justifies the cost of the damper. Adjustment types range from one-way adjustable dampers, which adjust bump and rebound together at a fixed ratio. Two-way adjustable dampers, where bump and rebound can be adjusted separately. Three-way adjustable dampers, where high and low speed bump and rebound are adjustable. Four-way adjustable dampers, where high and low speed bump and high and low speed rebound are adjustable.

The low speed and standard bump and rebound controls the sprung mass and tunes roll and pitch. High speed bump and rebound controls the unsprung mass and tunes the reaction to kerbs and bumps. Due to this the car can be tuned to the requirements of the chassis and the track surface. Inside the damper, the valving can be changed "to tune the switchover period between the high and low-speed characteristics of the car" (Smith, 2013).

A damper with a built-in pressurised nitrogen cartridge has a better ability to not have cavitation (foaming/bubbles) of the oil. This is caused by the oil "accelerating quickly and the gas pressure chamber (if present) does not equalise the pressure differential on either side of the piston" (Smith, 2013). This can decrease the damping forces which can make the handling of the vehicle inconsistent.

The most common type of damper in high end racing is the gas-filled monotube damper. This is usually pair with an external reservoir. "Through-rod dampers are also considered to be very good but have not been seen to be worth the extra cost over the previously mentioned dampers" (Smith, 2013).

The common, cheap dampers tend to be twin-tube damper. When twin-tube dampers are worked hard cavitation can occur. Cavitation is when oil and air are mixed together and causes the oil to "foam" up. This can give unreliable damping which is unwanted in performance vehicles.

Monotube dampers are beneficial due to "the volume of oil that is exposed to the outer wall of the damper and so can often cool better" (Smith, 2013). A monotube damper that is gas filled has got a high-pressure chamber of nitrogen, located at the bottom of the damper. This is known as a gas reservoir. This makes it difficult for the oil to cavitate, which makes it a more consistent damper. Monotube dampers can be seen on applications such as pull/push rod suspension systems. The rod and piston are pushed inside the damper; the piston there is ports and shims which restricts the flow of oil trying to pass through the piston. There is a bleed port that allows oil to pass through the shaft and piston. This allows oil to bypass the piston and shims.

External reservoirs on dampers allow for more oil to be carried. This allows for an increased cooling capacity and decreased unsprung weight, due to being mounted on the chassis.

Adjustability can be controlled accurately. The differences between a monotube damper and a monotube damper with an external reservoir are that there is $\frac{1}{2}$" to $\frac{3}{4}$" of adjustment. The rebound adjuster is a needle valve, along with having a transfer pipe. The transfer pipe can be a flexible braided line or a solid fixed mounted external reservoir on the side of the damper. External reservoir dampers also have got a compression adjuster on the chamber.

An inerter damper (also known as a mass damper or J-damper) is a concept from Malcolm Smith, linking electronic principles to mechanical principles. The force is the equivalent of current and velocity is equivalent to voltage. This provides a way of controlling the energy produced by the suspension and tyre deflection. The advantage is providing increased mechanical grip when compared to any other form of system; by controlling contact patch load variation. This system replaces the third damper system. "It uses a threaded rod that slides through a mass to transform the linear motion of the rod into rotary motion in the mass" (Homebuiltairplanes.com, 2013). The inertia of the mass creates a force which opposes the motion of the rod "that is proportional to the relative acceleration of the mass and the rod" (Homebuiltairplanes.com, 2013). The equation for an ideal inerter is $F = B \times (AA - AB)$. B is inertance (kg).

There are multiple ways to adjust compression on dampers (Penske dampers are used for these examples). On the 8100 series the compression adjuster is located in the remote reservoir assembly. It uses a CD Drum, which has six settings as seen in Figure 28. One being the softest (largest hole) and six being the stiffest (smallest hole). This is a common form of adjustment seen on dampers. The 8760 Series dampers have low speed and high-speed compression adjustments. Low speed compression, for example, is cornering. High speed compression, for example, are bumps. On the low speed compression adjuster, the oil is fed through an adjustable needle and jet assembly. Shutting down the flow of oil will restrict it, making low speed situations feel stiffer. This has approximately "30 clicks" (Penskeshocks.com, 2016) of adjustment. On the high-speed adjuster "the oil is forced to bypass the low speed needle and jet due to the fact that the small orifice in the jet causes the oil to hydraulic" (Penskeshocks.com, 2016). This forces the oil through another piston which orifices are covered by another shim shack, which is preloaded with force from the CD cage and shims, which makes it harder for the oil to flex the shims. There are 21+/- clicks of high-speed adjustment.

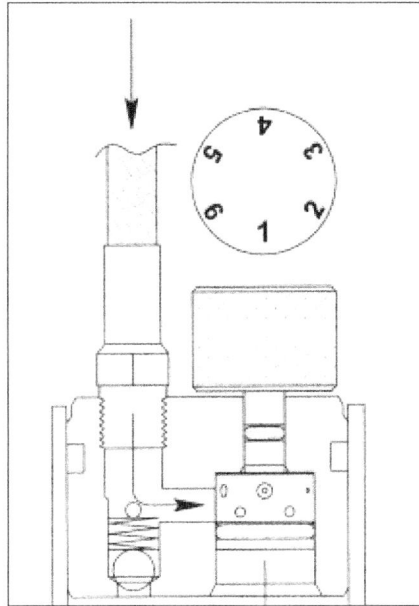

Figure 28 - Compression Adjustment (8100 Series)

(Penskeshocks.com, 2016)

Rebound adjustment on the 8100 Series can be found in the eyelet on the bottom of the main shaft. There is an adjustment screw that is used to control rebound. The 8760 Series is in a similar location. The needle is forced into the jet when the screw is turned clockwise. This restricts the oil, stiffening rebound. The opposite happens when the screw is turned counter clockwise.

N-post rig is used to test the dampers on a vehicle. This type of test is beneficial due to the car being tested with it, therefore the weight of the car will be on the dampers. This gives it an accurate demonstration of a vehicle being on track with all types of suspension movements. It can run the dampers through a series of tests, from damper potentiometers or increasing waves of increasing frequency and diminishing amplitude. It is also possible to measure contact patch load variation as well with this system; the lower the variation the better. This test can be more advantageous due to being able to test tyre warming index, ride quality, coupling between heave and roll, natural frequency, suspension motion ratios and damping ratios of heave and roll. Vertical hub acceleration can also be tested. An N-post rig set up is shown in Figure 29.

Figure 29 - N-Post Rig

(Moog.com, 2016)

The damper dynamometer was used to gain graphs of a damper's performance. The dynamometer used was a SPA BTP 2000. The damper tested was a Protech monotube damper. Figure 30 shows the inside on the damper dynamometer. An explanation of how the damper dynamometer will be to set up and used will be explained. Useful equations given in the manual are:

Peak Velocity = Radius (m) × Angular Velocity (rad per s)

Angular Velocity = 2 × π × Motor Frequency (Hz)

When mounting the damper, the dynamometer must be parked. The clevises must be threaded onto the load cell and input shaft. The crossbar must be un-clamped and raised to allow clearance to fit the damper and re-clamp. The damper is then fitted to the upper clevis, where the load cell is located. A pin is slid through the bearing, which is rotated to lock the clevis down. The crossbar is then un-clamped where the damper is lowered onto the lower clevis. The pin is slid through the bearing and rotated to lock the clevis down. The damper is slightly compressed using the crossbar in order to protect the damper during testing. The crossbar is then secured. Then temperature sensor is then attached to the body of the damper. The damper is then adjusted to the settings wanted. (Spa-uk.co.uk, 2016)

A set of procedures and operating conditions that the damper will be tested to are set. The maximum speed, minimum speed, number of data points and temperature will be in put into the software. A new test is started by clicking on Sample on the top bar, followed by Method, and then New. A test name will be asked for. Going onto the next stage is the Pre-run window, which asks if the damper is going to be warmed up before the test. This includes speed and the target temperature. The next window is what component is being tested, Shock or Spring, in this case a shock. The next window shows the speed type; multiple speed is a common test due to being able to view the graphs with the damper performing at multiple speeds. The next window shows selecting the speeds for the test. Stating the start and end speed (in inches per second) and using the equal speed steps option allows the software to calculate the individual speed steps by itself. The next window is selecting the gains for the test. This is the resolution of the test. The next window is the sample window, stating how many cycles the test will go through. Sample time is best set to automatic. The next window is the post-run procedures, in which park after running should be selected, along with parking in BDC. Finish is clicked and this method will be saved onto the computer. (Spa-uk.co.uk, 2016)

The test is able to be started from now. This is started by clicking Sample on the top bar and pressing on Start. The method just saved will have to be selected. The traces window will come up where a trace name can be entered. The load cell must be zeroed at this point. Once finish is clicked the test will start. During the test the mouse must be hovering over the abort test button, just in case any problems occur during the test. (Spa-uk.co.uk, 2016)

After the test has been completed the results can be reviewed. The results can be opened by toolbar shortcuts at the top of the software. The results of the tests are shown in Figures 31-35.

Figure 30 - Damper Dyno Motor

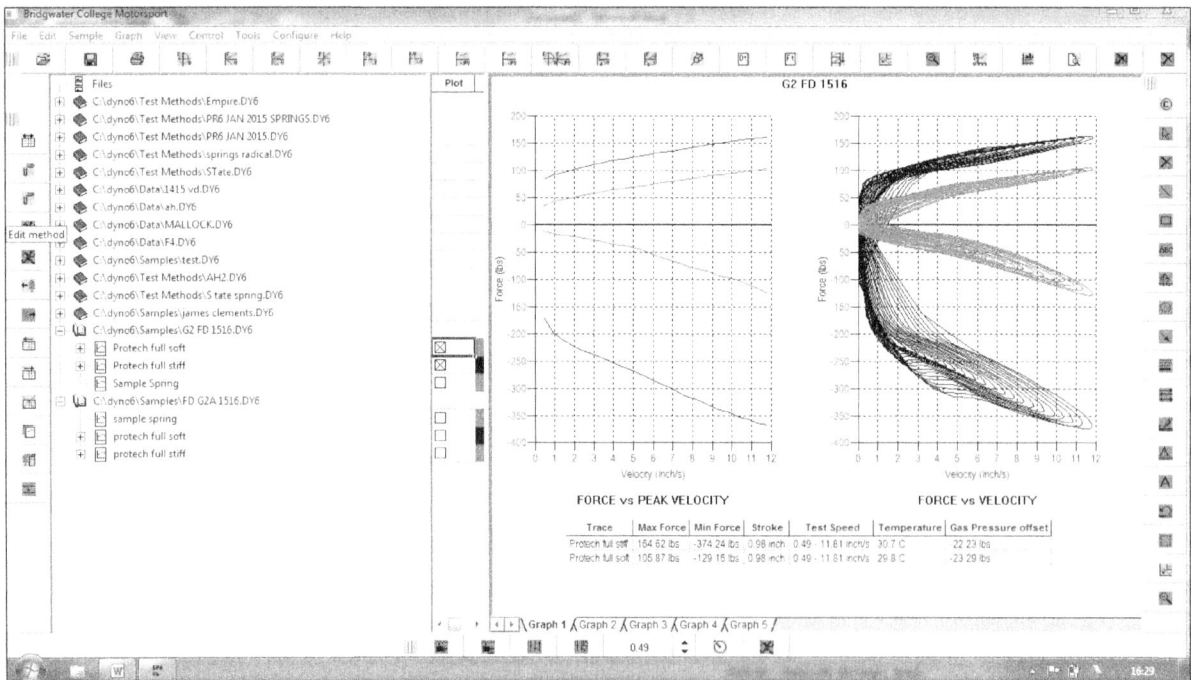

Figure 31 - Damper Dyno Results - Summary

Figure 31 shows the damper dynamometer results summary graph. The red line(s) are the damper in soft, and the black line(s) show the damper in stiff. This shows

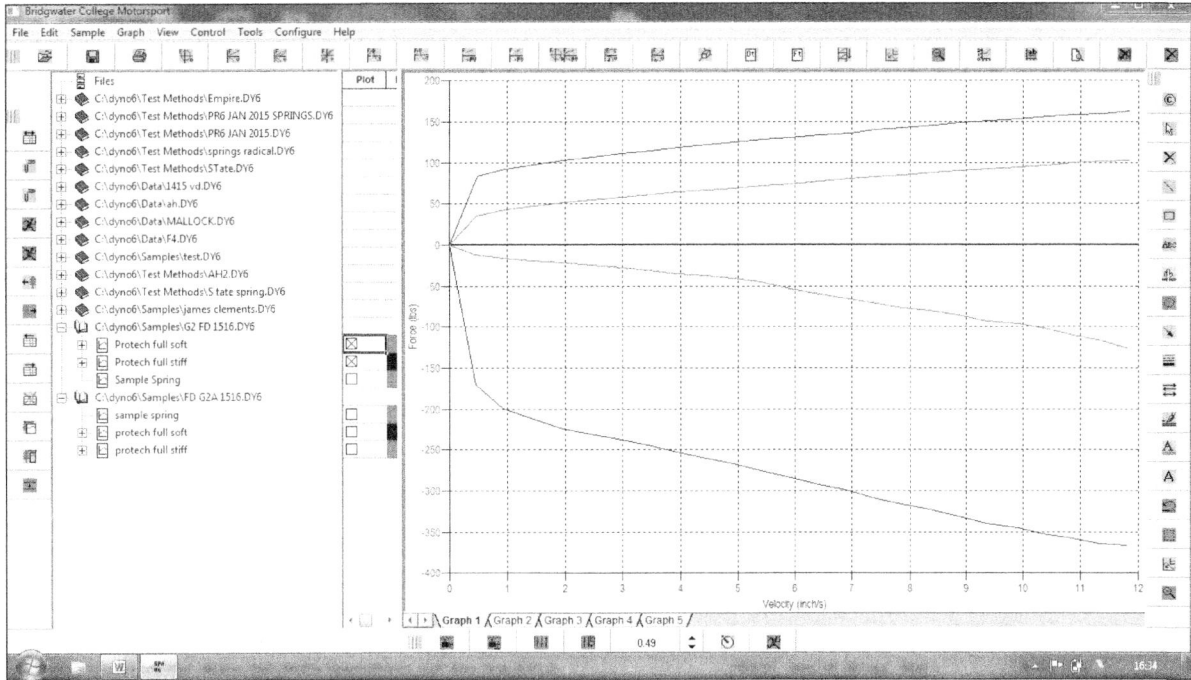

Figure 32 - Damper Dyno Results - Force vs Peak Velocity Extended to Zero

Figure 32 shows the damper dynamometer results for the force vs peak velocity extended to zero graph. The red line is the damper in soft, and the black line shows the damper in stiff. This shows

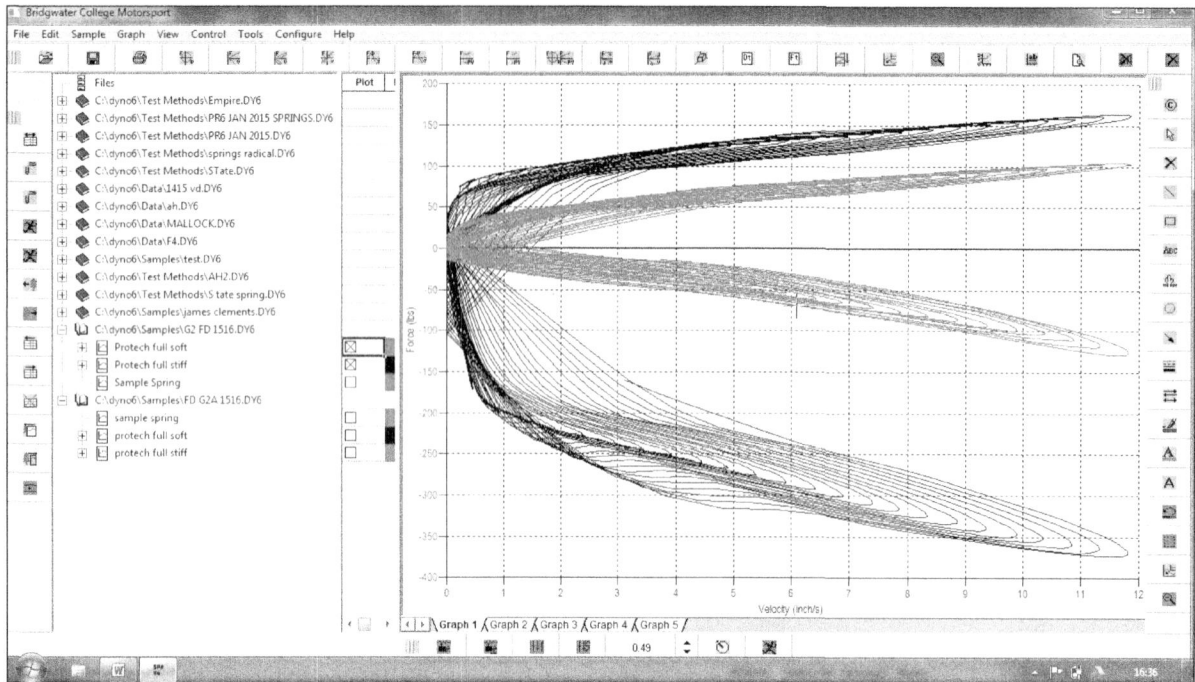

Figure 33 - Damper Dyno Results - Force vs Velocity

Figure 33 shows the damper dynamometer results for force vs velocity graph. The red lines are the damper in soft, and the black lines show the damper in stiff. This shows the damper accelerating and decelerating. Positive is bump and the negative is rebound. The level of hysteresis is due to the increase of fluid inertia and dynamic operating pressure. It shows the amount of force in lbs to move the damper a certain velocity.

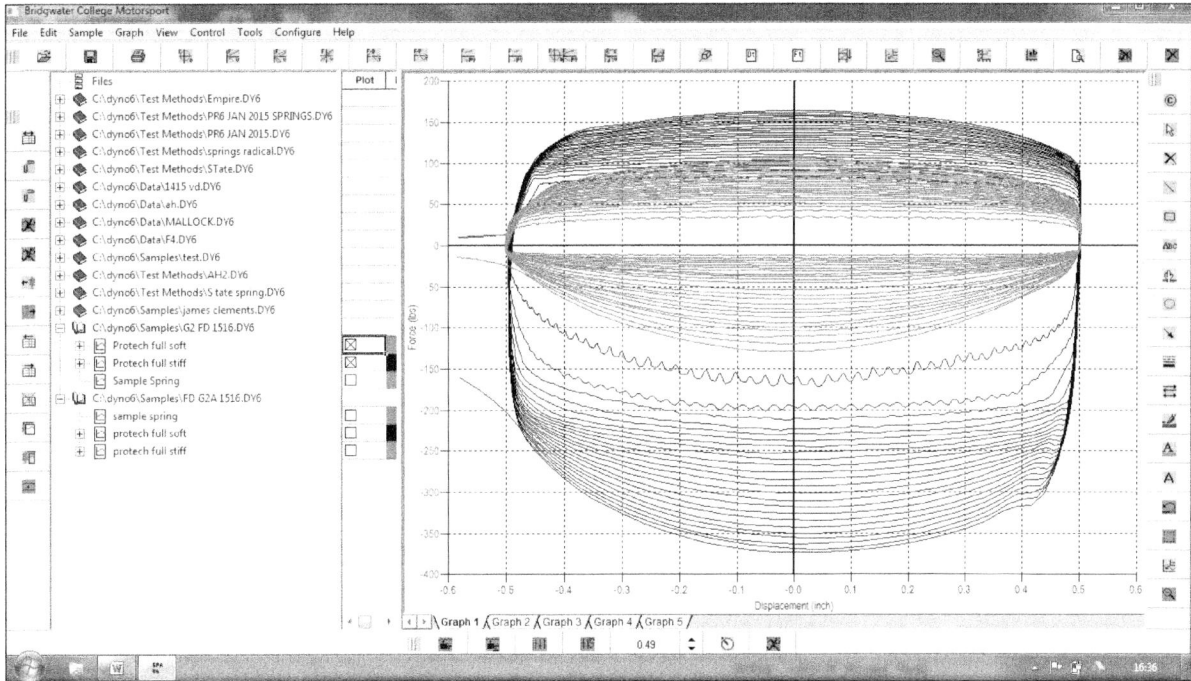

Figure 34 - Damper Dyno Results - Force vs Displacement

Figure 34 shows the damper dynamometer results for force vs displacement graph. The red lines are the damper in soft, and the black lines show the damper in stiff. This shows

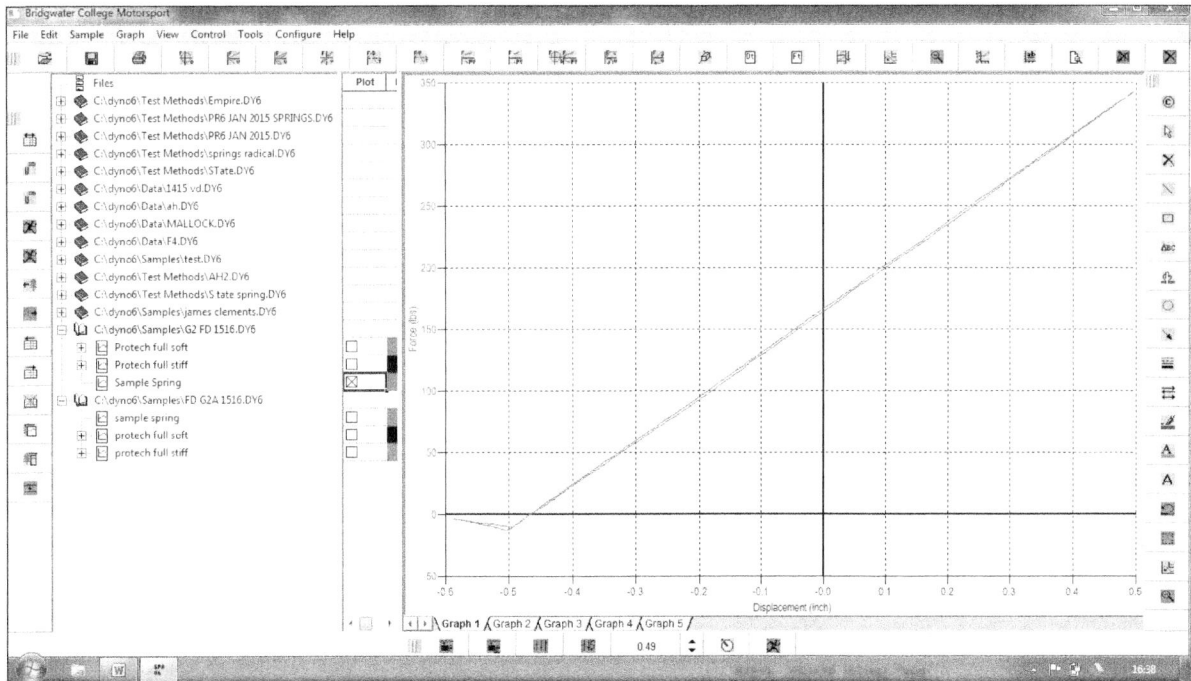

Figure 35 - Damper Dyno Results - Spring

Figure 35 shows the damper dynamometer results for the spring graph. This shows force by displacement of a spring that has been tester on the dynamometer.

4.0 Race Car Set-Up

This section of the study shows how to carry out a base set up on a race car in order to perform at its optimum for a dry circuit. Demonstrating the ability of setting up a performance car for use and identifying its suitability to race.

4.1 Set-Up & Tracking

This section is a task to record and analyse the current vehicle settings, from the analysis, make the necessary adjustments to the car detailing why the adjustments are necessary, how they are made and what effect this will have on the vehicle dynamics.

This practical task was performed on a Swift 2000 Formula Ford. This task is to carry out a geometry check and to corner weight this vehicle. The first task carried out on the vehicle was a chassis inspection. The chassis inspection includes checking the condition of the wishbones, rod ends, suspension mounting points, wheel bearings and other similar areas. This inspection showed that on the front of the vehicle, the steering rack bushes were different sizes, inner track rods had different bolts, along with the top of the dampers having different bolts. On the front right there were some damaged drive pegs. On the rear of the vehicle there were some missing washers and top hats on both sides of the rocker arms, along with drive pegs being damaged on both sides. On the rear left of the vehicle the damper was missing a top hat. The inspection also came up with all the rocker arms being slightly bent, but due to their construction this is expected.

The next stage of the process is to set the tyre pressures to their hot pressure. This would be 21 psi. Once the tyre pressures were set the rear anti-roll bar (ARB) was disconnected. After this was completed the ride height was measured (Figures 36 & 37). Ride height is measured from the lowest point of the chassis, front and rear. Preload was then set (the load used to move the spring). This was done by measuring the spring length in position, then unwinding it fully open and loose. It was set to 375 lbs/inch (Figure 39 & 40). The ground clearance for the Swift was 52 mm. Ground clearance is measured from the lowest point of the car, as shown in Figure 38. The ride height measured:

RH (L)	RH (R)
71.5 mm	73 mm
62 mm	65 mm

Figure 36 - Measuring Front Ride Height

Figure 37 - Measuring Rear Ridge Height

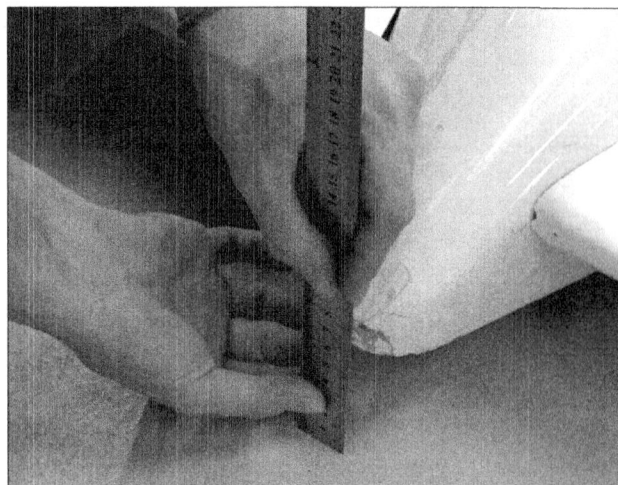

Figure 38 - Measuring Ground Clearance

Figure 39 - Preload

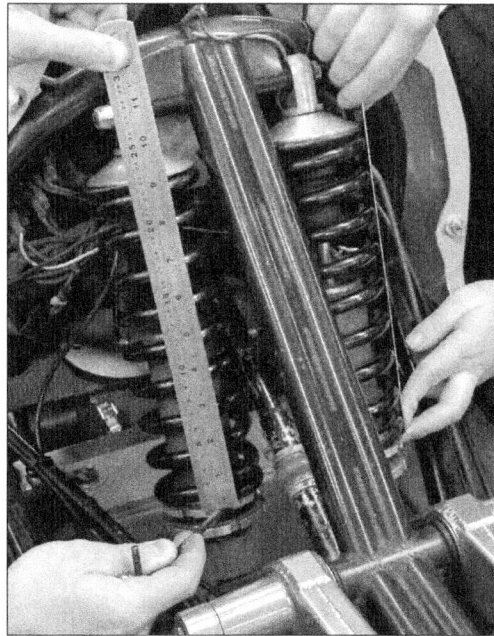

Figure 40 - Measuring Preload

From the results given by the ride height it can be seen that there is negative rake, due to the rear being lower than the front. This must be changed as it is losing downforce. This changed to having 70 mm front ride height and 75mm rear ride height, which was done by twisting the drop links on the Swift for the front, as shown in Figure 41. the rear ride height was adjusted by winding in the spring. The preload was set by measuring the spring length (which is accurate) or can also be done by measuring the turns/clicks. After each adjustment the suspension was settled.

Figure 41 - Ride Height Adjustments

4.1.1 Original Alignment Measurements

The caster, camber, toe and thrust angle measurements were recorded in order to see where the vehicle was before any geometry changed were made. The original measurements were:

Caster (FL)	Caster (FR)
6.1°	5.2°

Camber (L)	Camber (R)
-0.8°	-1.4°
-0.6°	-0.7°

Toe (L)	Toe (R)
20 mm	1 mm
5 mm	-2.5 mm

Thrust Angle (L)	Thrust Angle (R)
5.5	2.2
7	7

4.1.2 Caster

Caster is only on the front wheels. Caster is measured by having turn plates underneath the front wheels, with a camber gauge, set on the caster setting, on the wheel. The wheel is then turned inside 10°. The camber gauge is set to zero, the wheel is then returned back to centre then bought outside 10°. The gauge shows the caster reading in degrees. The caster angle improves the vehicles stability as it helps with self-centring. Caster is always positive, shown in Figure 42, and gives a dynamic camber change. It gives negative camber on the outside wheel while giving positive camber on the inside wheel. Caster is always the same on both sides of the front wheel and is usually seen in the range or 4° to 8°.

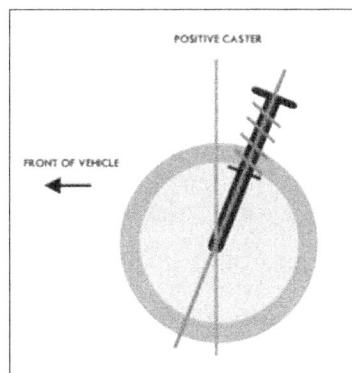

Figure 42 - Positive Caster

(Vikingspeedshop.com, 2016)

4.1.3 Camber

Camber is measured on all wheels, straight ahead with the camber gauge on the wheels, on the camber setting. The reading shown on the screen is the amount of camber in degrees. Usually camber is always negative, due to the tyre rolling onto itself while cornering. Camber is usually set at the same value both sides, but it can be set unequal depending on circuit direction, circuit characteristics, determined by tyre temperatures. Due to the Swift's tyres being cross ply the range of camber is smaller than on radial tyres. This range is 0.5° to -1° (Startline.org.uk, 2016). There is usually more negative camber on the front wheels when compared to the rear. Figure 43 shows positive and negative camber.

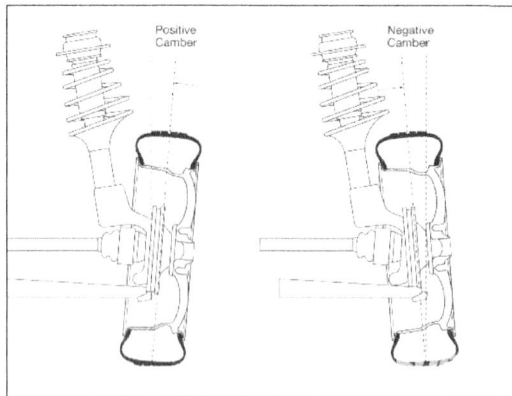

Figure 43 - Camber

(Allon White, 2016)

4.1.4 Toe

Toe, again, is measured on all wheels on the vehicle. Usually the front wheels run toe out, while the rear wheels run toe in. Toe in allows for better stability as the wheels are physically pointing inwards. Toe does create some rolling resistance; this has to be kept in mind when increasing any amount of toe. Toe out on the front wheels allows for a good initial turn in, but the front can become to dart with a tendency to wander, reacts more to bumps and undulations. Toe out is usually run at 1mm – 2mm. Figure 44 shows an example of toe in and toe out.

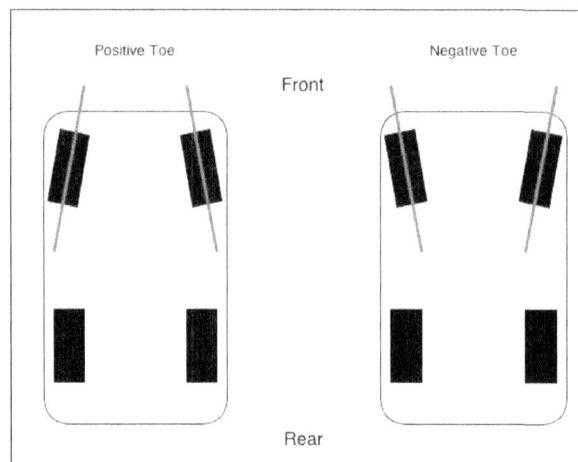

Figure 44 - Toe

(Leakylugnut.com, 2016)

4.1.5 Thrust Angle

Thrust angle is the angle the vehicle is travelling down the road. An incorrect thrust angle will mean that the vehicle would "crab" down the road, as shown in Figure 45. This is a problem for aerodynamic devices as the air is hitting the devices at a different yaw angle than what the vehicle is travelling.

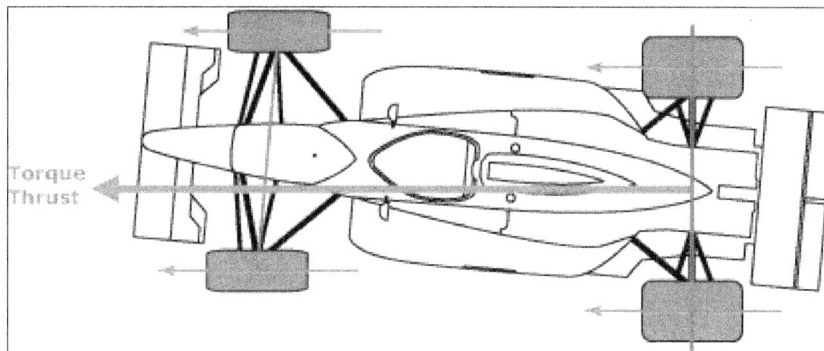

Figure 45 - Thrust Angle

(Tirerack.com, 2016)

4.1.6 Rear Alignment

The rear geometry was carried out next. This "must be done with the car in a race-ready state. This means it should be full of fluids with half race fuel in the tank (as an average fuel load) and the driver" (Smith, 2013). Camber adjustments are first carried out, then toe and thrust angle. The camber was measured to be with the camber gauge; on the left $-0.6°$ and $-0.7°$ on the right. For cross-ply tyres the ideal camber on the rear is $-0.5°$, this is due to the construction of cross-ply tyres. The rear camber is adjusted by increasing/decreasing length of the lower wishbone barrel nuts closest to the hub. Toe was next to be measured and then adjusted. The original measurements for toe were 5 mm on the left and -2.5 mm on the right on the right (Figure 46). This gives a combined rear toe on 2.5 mm toe in. On the rear the toe measurement is read backwards, if it shows 2 mm toe out it represents 2 mm toe in. This needs to be changed to 3 mm toe in across the axle, 1.5 mm toe in on each wheel. Toe is changed on the Swift by changing the length of the lower wishbone rod ends connected to the hub in ratio to each other. The rear axle thrust angle was next to be carried out. The flags on the front wheels indicate the direction of where the rear wheels are facing. To get the thrust angle in line the flag must display the same number. The original measurements for thrust angle were 7 on the left and 5 on the right. Thrust angle is adjusted by the same rod ends used to change the toe angle, while looking at the flags on the front wheels (Figure 47).

Figure 46 - Rear Toe

Figure 47 - Rear Thrust Angle

4.1.7 Front Alignment

The front geometry was next to be carried out. On the front caster is always carried out first, followed by camber, then toe and the flags. Caster was carried out by putting the front wheels onto turn plates, turning the wheel inside to 10°, caster gauge set to zero and wheel turned back to zero and to 10° outside (Figure 48). This was carried out on both wheels. Caster was changed by turning the lower rear wishbone rod end. Caster was changed to 5.4° on the left and 5.6° on the right, the 0.2° difference is acceptable. Camber was adjusted by turning the barrel nut on the bottom wishbone connected to the hub. Camber was adjusted to -1° on the left and -0.7° on the right, the 0.3° difference is acceptable. Toe was adjusted by twisting the track rod. Toe was adjusted to -1.5mm on the left and 1.5mm on the right, giving 0mm of toe across the axle. Thrust angle was adjusted by turning both track rod ends the same amount (to keep the same amount of toe) to the same numbers on the flags on the rear tyres.

Figure 48 - Castor Measurement

4.1.8 Corner Weighting

Corner weighting was to be completed next. Corner weights show the weight of the vehicle at the individual corners. This can be useful as the cross weight of vehicle could be incorrect, meaning that the cornering ability of the vehicle is decreased, as the car will be trying to pivot itself on the lightest wheel. The corner weights were set out in front of all the wheels, set at the same height and level. Having the scales at the same height and level eliminates incorrect readings by having the weight "pushed" over to one side by a scale higher than the others. Having the scales level means that the weight is spread even all over the scale. The scales are made level with spirt levels and raised/lowered to the same height with a reference and laser. Once the Swift was rolled onto the scales it was possible to see the weights of each corner and the cross weight on the screen (Figure 49). It was possible to change the weights of each corner, thus the cross weight, by adjusting the drop links on the Swift, giving the weights as shown in Figure 50.

Figure 49 - Corner Weights Before Adjustment

Figure 50 - Corner Weights After Adjustment

4.1.9 Pre-Set Up Sheet

The pre-set-up sheet is used to record all the alignment information before changes have been made. Figure 51 shows this.

Pre-Set Up

Date	11/02/2016
Vehicle	Swift 2000
Event	Post Chassis Set Up

Tyre Pressure	21 psi		Tyre Pressure	21 psi
Castor (°)	6.1		Castor (°)	5.2
Camber (°)	-0.8		Camber (°)	-1.4
Toe (mm)	7		Toe (mm)	11
Thrust Angle	5.5		Thrust Angle	2.2
Ride Height (mm)	71.5		Ride Height (mm)	73
Corner Weight (kg)	95		Corner Weight (kg)	66
Cross Weight (kg)	56.9%		Cross Weight (kg)	

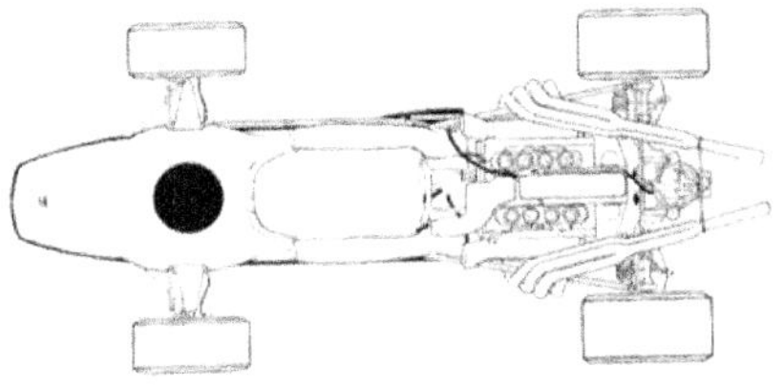

Tyre Pressure	21 psi		Tyre Pressure	21 psi
Camber (°)	-0.6		Camber (°)	-0.7
Toe (mm)	5		Toe (mm)	-2.5
Thrust Angle	7		Thrust Angle	5
Ride Height (mm)	62		Ride Height (mm)	65
Corner Weight (kg)	130		Corner Weight (kg)	159.5
Cross Weight (kg)			Cross Weight (kg)	56.9%
			Total Weight (kg)	450.5

Figure 51 - Pre-Set Up Sheet

4.1.10 Post-Set Up Sheet

The post-set up sheet is used to record all the alignment information after changes have been made, Figure 52 shows this.

Post-Set Up

Date	25/02/2016
Vehicle	Swift 2000
Event	Post Chassis Set Up

Front Left:

Tyre Pressure	21 psi
Castor (°)	5.4
Camber (°)	-1
Toe (mm)	-1.5
Thrust Angle	5.5
Ride Height (mm)	70
Corner Weight (kg)	80.5
Cross Weight (kg)	225.5 (50.1%)

Front Right:

Tyre Pressure	21 psi
Castor (°)	5.6
Camber (°)	-0.7
Toe (mm)	1.5
Thrust Angle	2.2
Ride Height (mm)	70
Corner Weight (kg)	80.5
Cross Weight (kg)	

Rear Left:

Tyre Pressure	21 psi
Camber (°)	-0.5
Toe (mm)	-1.5
Thrust Angle	7
Ride Height (mm)	75
Corner Weight (kg)	144.5
Cross Weight (kg)	

Rear Right:

Tyre Pressure	21 psi
Camber (°)	-0.5
Toe (mm)	-1.5
Thrust Angle	7
Ride Height (mm)	75
Corner Weight (kg)	145
Cross Weight (kg)	225.5 (50.1%)
Total Weight (kg)	450.5

Figure 52 - Post-Set Up Sheet

4.2 Race Car's Readiness to Race

For the same vehicle an inspection detailing its readiness to race is carried out. Listing and showing evidence of the inspections carried out on the vehicles steering, suspension, wheels and tyres detailing their suitability to race and recommendations in order to rectify any problems.

It is important to check a vehicles readiness to race. Doing this check can show parts of the vehicle that need repairing or replacing in order to be save for the driver to race. The main areas of inspection are the steering, suspension, tyres and wheels. Other areas to look at are fluids, such as brake and clutch fluid, throttle linkages, brake discs and pads.

Two of these checks were carried out, on the college Swift and the college Van Diemen. The results of these inspections were:

Van Diemen –

LF	RF
Tyre: 66 Shore hardness	Tyre: 70 Shore hardness
Lower wishbone bent	Upper wishbone upright bolt
Lower hub rose joint needs adjusting	Four bolts loose
Tie rod bent	Track rod bolt (closed to steering rack)-
Track rod (rack) missing washer	wrong size
Rack bushes	Lower wishbone bent
Track rod washer different	More steering lock than left
	Tie rod bent
	Rack bushes
	Track rod washer different
LR	RR
Tyre: 67 Shore hardness	Tyre: 69 Shore hardness
New split pins for brakes	Upper wishbone upright bolt
Anti-roll bar loose	Brake line not secure
Lower wishbone small bend & dent	New split pins for brakes
Brake pads	Rocker bent
	Brake pads

Other areas found during the Van Diemen inspection were that the steering wheel was worn, the clutch slave cylinder needed replacing and the brakes needed adjusting due to the very hard brake pedal.

Swift –

LF	RF
Tyre: 86 Shore hardness	Tyre: 82 Shore hardness
Steering rack bushes different sizes	Steering rack bushes different sizes
Inner track rods different bolts	Inner track rods different bolts
Top of dampers different bolts	Top of dampers different bolts
	Drive peg
LR	**RR**
Tyre: 80 Shore hardness	Tyre: 85 Shore hardness
Drive peg	Drive peg
Damper missing top hat	Rocker arms missing washers & top hats
Rocker arms missing washers & top hats	

Other areas found during the inspection on the Swift were that the throttle sticks when fully open, worn steering wheel, top up front brake fluid, all rocker arms slightly bent (due to their construction this is expected).

The conclusion of these inspections is that both of these vehicles are not in an acceptable condition to race. This is due to many serious faults with the cars found during the inspection. These serious faults include; the Shore hardness of the tyres being too high. Incorrect bolts in vital components, this could mean that the bolts could fail, putting the driver in serious danger. Damaged, or missing bushes, meaning that the handling of the vehicle will have a different compliance when compared to new bushes.

4.3 Handling Characteristics of a Single Seater Race Car

This section considers the handling characteristics of a single seater performance car, demonstrate in detail using diagrams and calculations how the layout, suspension, steering and tyres have an effect on the handling and dynamic stability of the vehicle under straight line and cornering conditions.

A single seater performance car is known for being a fast race car. This is due to its very good handling characteristics. The is due to many reasons, such as, the layout of the vehicle. This can be seen visually due to its symmetrical layout, as seen in Figure 53. Due to this symmetrical layout the weight distribution of a single seater is very good. The left to right weight distribution is nearly always 50/50 (50% of the weight on the left side of the vehicle and the other 50% on the other side), when the front to back weight distribution is usually 50/50 or 40/60. Because of this weight distribution it means that the vehicles centre of gravity is central to the vehicle, where the driver is situated. This means that the driver can feel every corner of the vehicle and know what is going on and where to place it on track. Due to the single seater design being very low to the ground it also means that the centre of gravity is very low as well, meaning greater cornering ability, thus resulting in quicker lap times.

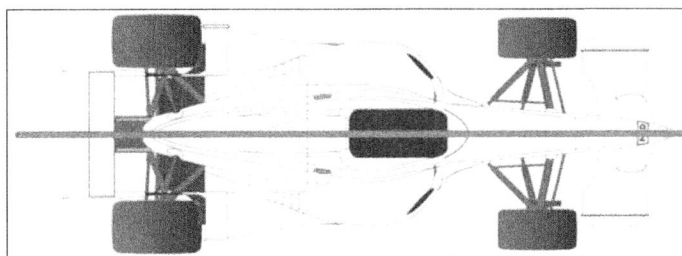

Figure 53 - Symmetry of a Single Seater

(Core77, 2016)

The stiffness of the chassis plays a key role within the single seater. Having a stiff chassis means that there is very little chassis movement resulting in a greater amount of feedback being given back to the driver. This allows the driver to have a greater feel of under/oversteer when it happens, therefore allowing the driver to correct earlier and quicker. The stiff chassis is gained by using a Monocoque or in lower end Motorsports a tubular chassis. These chassis' have low compliance, meaning the stiff chassis, due to the bush-less or the use of very hard bushes on the suspension. This allows for very little weight transfer when cornering.

The wishbone layout and design on a single seater is usually a double wishbone layout, while the suspension is inboard. This allows for a greater aerodynamic efficiency since the suspension is not in the freestream. A double wishbone layout also allows for "greater steering response as steering axis is separate to the vertical motion" (Balancemotorsport.co.uk, 2016), when compared to MacPherson Strut designs. The unsprung mass on a single seater is usually very low due to the inboard design. Unsprung mass being low allows for an improved contact patch between the tyre and the surface of the track. It helps with bumps, undulations, transitions and similar suspension movements. The allows the suspension to react faster due to the low inertia. Double wishbone suspension also allows for greater adjustability.

Due to the double wishbone design, roll centre is able to be controlled "within a limited range of motion" (Balancemotorsport.co.uk, 2016). It also has a more consistent location of roll centre.

The adjustability of components on a single seater also gives it the upper hand when compared to another race vehicle. Due to the suspension 'openness' it is possible to easily change alignment settings on the car, including caster, camber, toe, thrust angle, etc. This allows for quick changes to tracking when needed, such as at an event. Due to the variety of adjustment it is possible to set up a car 'perfectly' for a specific track, given a large advantage over competitors.

A single seater performance car has very little weight transfer. This causes each tyre to be evenly loaded (using the tyre to its maximum potential). Weight transfer occurs during braking, accelerating and cornering. The heavier the car the more weight transfer will occur. During cornering the weight will transfer to the outside tyre reducing the grip on the inside wheel. With a higher centre of gravity there is more weight transfer. Different wheelbase length can result in change in static weight distribution and can change weight transfer. With a wider track there can be less weight transfer. (Smith, 2013). The longitudinal weight transfer calculation is as shown:

$$\text{Longitudinal Weight Transfer} = \frac{\text{Accel G Force (g)} \times \text{CG (Inches)} \times \text{Total Weight (lbs)}}{\text{Wheelbase (Inches)}}$$

The anti-dive, anti-squat and anti-lift is the geometry that "controls the amount of pitch movement of the car by reducing the amount of load going through the suspension springs and placing a proportion of the load transfer through the suspension arms instead" (Smith, 2013). Dive is the nose diving under braking. Squat is the rear diving under heavy acceleration. Lift is when the front droops in acceleration and the rear dropping under braking. The equation for anti is as shown:

$$\text{Anti \%} = \tan\theta / (h \div l) \times 100$$

$$\tan 11.3 / (0.5 \div 2.5) \times 100 = 100\%$$

(Smith, 2013)

5.0 Race Car Suspension Systems

This section of the study discuss' the advantages and disadvantages of the different suspension actuation systems used on a competition car. This includes In/Outboard, Rocker Arm, Monoshock, pushrod, pull rod, 3-damper set ups and any other type deemed necessary.

There are many different suspension actuation systems used on competition vehicles. These suspension systems include double wishbone (inboard and outboard), MacPherson Strut, pushrod/pull rod, Monoshock and a 3-damper set up.

5.1 Double Wishbone

Double wishbone suspension is a very common suspension system on high end performance road vehicles and competition vehicles. This is due to its compact and simple design. When the suspension is in bump or droop the camber of the wheel does not change, if the arms are the equal in length, but when this comes to a corner the camber does change. To stop this a short upper arm is used, when the suspension goes into bump the wheel gets an increase in negative camber, helping cornering. Many double wishbone suspension systems are unequal, when corning the inside wheel has got positive chamber and the outside wheel has got negative chamber; giving maximum contact patch onto the ground, thus increasing cornering stability. It is a very versatile suspension system as the dampers can be set outboard or inboard depending on the application. The negatives of this suspension are that it tends to be "more expensive than other variants of suspension and there are a greater number of parts in this system, which can take longer to work on" (Double Wishbone Suspension - Explained, 2012). Figure 54 shows an example of double wishbone suspension.

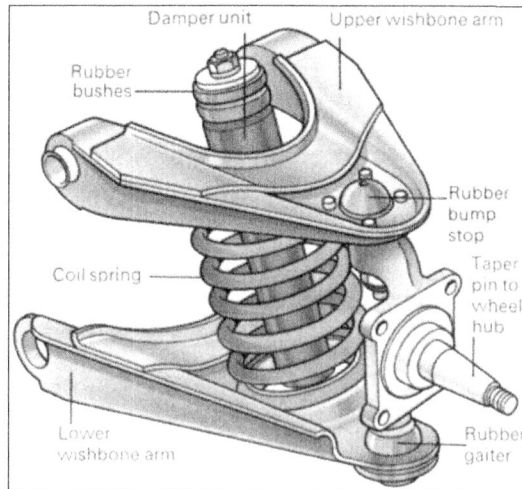

Figure 54 - Double Wishbone Suspension

(Unique Cars and Parts, 2016)

5.2 Outboard

Outboard suspension on a double wishbone suspension system is preferred for high end road vehicles, this is due to its simplicity, it ease of placement and that the damper and spring would not be in the freestream, thus causing drag. On the other hand, if a single seater uses an outboard double wishbone suspension system the damper oil is cooled due to the colder air passing it during driving. Due to the damper and spring being located onto the wishbones it means that it increases the unsprung weight by a large amount, this reduces the contact between the tyre and the surface of the road. Having a lower unsprung weight gives lower inertia; faster reacting suspension during bumps, undulations and transitions. As mentions it is detrimental to the airflow passing the suspension and creates turbulent air behind it. Due to its location the mass it not central and it does not allow for adjustment in preload and ride height. It is also difficult to alter the motion ratio; the relationship between a system that involves linkages whereby there is a difference in displacement between one end of a pivot and the opposing side. An example of outboard double wishbone suspension is shown in Figure 54.

5.3 Inboard

Inboard suspension on a double wishbone suspension system is preferred for single seater performance cars. This design uses a rocker arm to attach to the damper. Due to the dampers and springs being covered allowing for a more aerodynamic design for open wheeled vehicles. The damper and spring are more central to the vehicle, giving a more central mass when compared to an outboard design, and giving the design a lower unsprung weight. Another positive to the design is the ability in the design to select the motion ratio. The downsides of the inboard design include that a gas filled monotube damper must be used, as it cannot be cooled, and oil filled dampers temperature get higher. There is a small increase in weight in this design and it raises the centre of gravity due to the dampers and springs being on top of the driver's legs. Figure 55 shows an example of inboard double wishbone suspension layout.

Figure 55 - Inboard Double Wishbone Suspension

(Tamiya, 2016)

5.4 MacPherson Strut

MacPherson Strut suspension is commonly seen on road cars, usually front wheel drive. This suspension is a cheap and light option for many car manufactures and comes in a narrow package when compared to many other suspension systems but has a taller design than many other systems. Negatives also include having small amounts of camber change with body roll, with no camber gain while cornering and this design must be connected to a body, which is why when body roll occurs the camber changes. MacPherson Strut's need to be mounted to a uni-body due to the stress and forces created by the strut, but due to most road cars already being uni-body it is a popular design. Figure 56 shows a simple diagram of a MacPherson Sturt.

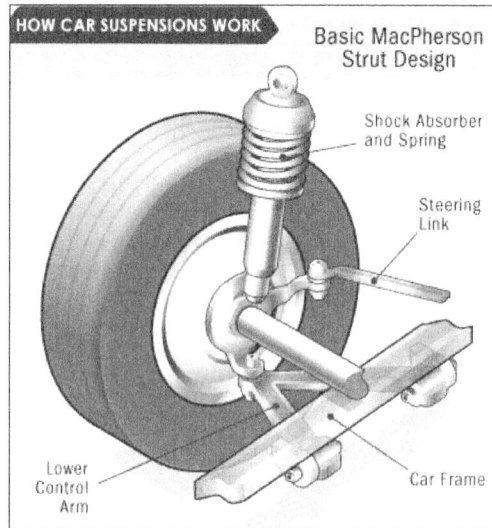

Figure 56 - MacPherson Strut

(How Car Suspensions Work, 2005)

5.5 Push/Pull Rod

Push rod suspension can be seen in Formula One cars. It uses a double wishbone suspension. When the tyre hits a bump it pushes the pushrod, which in turn pivots a rocker, which turns a torsion bar which gives resistance. The rocker also compresses a damper along with a spring. This spring is a heave spring, which is connected to both rockers either side. This provides extra force when both tyres go into bump. This keeps the body elevated. The anti-roll bar pivots in between both sides of the torsion bar, meaning when cornering one tyre will be rising, in turn raising the other tyre bringing the car down. Advantages include restricting wheel movement keeping the car very stiff. This means that there is little to no body roll and the constant raising and lowering of ride height, meaning that the aerodynamics of the car is kept at a constant. Due to push rods inboard design it is a low drag system. This system allows for motion ratio design freedom and give ride height and preload independence. The disadvantages to push rod suspension set ups are usually expensive and complex. A diagram of this description of push rod suspension is shown in Figure 57.

Pull rod suspension is similar to push rod but appears to be flipped upside down. Instead of the push rod going from the lower wishbone up, a pull rod goes from the upper wishbone down into the body of the vehicle. When bump occurs the pull rod pivots a rocker, in turn twisting a torsion bar, and pushing a damper and spring. The benefits to pull rod suspension are the same as push rod apart from pull rod suspension has got a lower centre of gravity since all the components of the suspension system are situated lower down in the vehicle. Disadvantages include the expense on the system, complexity and that push rod suspension supports the weight of the car, which means that the upper wishbone is supporting a lot of the weight, meaning that it usually has to be strengthened, usually increasing weight. Pull rod suspension can be seen being used in the Ferrari F2012 Formula One car (Figure 58).

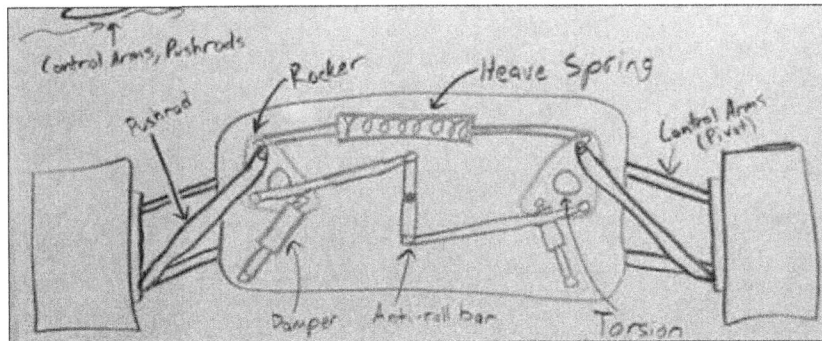

Figure 57 - Push Rod Suspension

(Pushrod Suspension - Explained, 2012)

Figure 58 - Pull Rod Suspension

(Ferrari F2012, 2012)

5.6 Monoshock

A monoshock suspension system uses a single damper/spring set up. It uses a push or pull rod system, paired with a common rocker, "mounted on a base plate on the chassis and able to move laterally and rotate around a lateral axis" (Smith, 2013). "Either side of the common rocker is a Belleville spring stack" (Smith, 2013). When roll occurs the rocker moves sideways, while the spring controls the roll. When bump or rebound occurs the "rocker rotates and actuates the sole spring/damper unit, which is mounted at one end to the common rocker and the chassis at the other" (Smith, 2013).

Benefits of a monoshock suspension system is that there are separate roll and pitch rates, which are infinitely tuneable. Many ways to configure the Belleville stack, "based on spring type and orientation and the preload added to them" (Smith, 2013). The weight of this set up is low, along with being small so packaging is easier. This set up is not seen on the rear of a vehicle due to problems with grip that happens with an undamped, stiff set up.

5.7 Third Damper

The third damper set up is an anti-heave system that "can also be used to control aerodynamic downforce affecting the ride height of the car" (Smith, 2013).

6.0 Basics of Vehicle Dynamics

A question you may ask yourself; what can affect the dynamics of a vehicle? The list below shows all a vehicles characteristic that affect vehicle dynamics: *Note: all highlighted characteristics have a major role in a vehicle driving dynamics. You may also notice that the same characteristics have effects on different roles and situations of the vehicle.*

Acceleration

- Power
- Torque
- Gearing
- Wheels/tyres
- Drivetrain
- Engine
- Weight
- Final drive
- Set up
- Rolling resistance
- Drag
- Rotational inertia
- Semi auto
- Weight distribution
- Mechanical efficiency

Braking

- Tyres
- Pads
- Discs
- Callipers
- Cooling
- Weight
- Set up

- Brake bias
  - Brakes
- Engine breaking
- Downforce/drag
- Weight distribution
- Centre of gravity

Cornering
- Tyres/wheels
  - Dampers
    - Set up
- Downforce
- Steering rack
  - Weight
- Differential characteristics
  - Weight distribution

Top speed
- Gearing
- Power
- Downforce/drag
  - Engine
  - Weight
  - Tyres
- Rolling resistance
  - Set up

Controllability & response
- Dampers
  - Set up
- Downforce

- Weight
  - Low un-sprung weight
    - Rack ratio
  - Centre of gravity height
- Rubber bushes (compliance) - removing excess compliance to gain response and feedback
  - Throttle mapping
  - Differential (load transfer characteristics)
    - Chassis stiffness
      - Tyres
    - Aero balance
  - Inertia and polar moment of inertia

The main characteristics are:
- Tyres/wheels
  - Suspension
    - Chassis
  - Handing and set up

6.1 Set Up & Design

Primary: modifications and design alterations that will only yield an improvement.
Expensive. For example: engine power, weight, CG, tyre compounds (optimised)
Secondary: tuning/balance change in order to make an improvement but will
come with a compromise
Engineering, cheaper. Spring rates, lift to drag ratio > adjustments, geometry, anti-roll bar, damping

Base set up > initial neutral car set up. Is a good starting point.

An instant lap time decrease

Tuning one area, most likely a decrease in performance for another area.

For example: add more camber > contact patch when cornering, less rolling resistance, helps tyre wear, provides camber thrust. But is less stable in a straight line, less traction, excess heat & load.

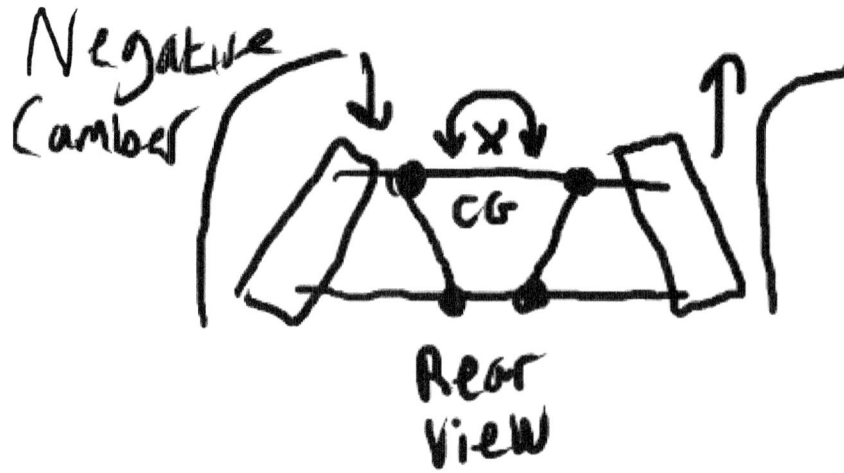

6.2 Stiffer Springs

Pros: More responsive in directional change, contact patch loading more even - across the axle, can run more aero and run lower ride height, less weight transfer through springs, stable ride heights and less roll

Cons: Poor wet performance, less compliance - bumps and undulations, less traction, harsher ride - more sensitive, on bumpy terrain tyres loosing contact, potentially less progressive

6.3 Top Speed

Pros: More top speed

Cons: Less acceleration on straight and corner exit, brakes

6.4 Downforce

Pros: Better cornering, more vertical load, more stability, better braking, better acceleration (tyre/power limited), heat generation

Cons: Drag - fuel usage, right height control, ^tyre wear, depends on driver ability

- The faster a car can corner (think G-G plot (think brake, entry, apex and exit)) the less time it spends in a given sector = quicker lap time

- If a car is able to exit the corner faster, it will be able to spend less time on the straight (higher average speed) = quicker lap time

6.5 Examples of Compromises

- F-duct (initial) with large fin > stalled wing for less downforce > fin made car sensitive in cross wind, driver had to move hand or leg to cover up duct
- Blown diffuser (initial) > gave more downforce but heat management issues had to be developed

Compromises, causes, effects and limitations - regulations, tools, understanding, financial

7.0 Wheels & Tyres

Wheel requirements:

- Strength and rigidity (materials)
- Cooling for the brake assembly
- Clearance between wheel and brake/suspension systems. Different manufacturers will use different rim cross-sectional patterns. Therefore, the same size wheel from a different manufacturer may not always fit.

7.1 Types & Materials

Split rims

Most commonly 3 piece - inner, centre and outer. Cast, forged and billet. Allows for alteration and ease of finding correct widths and offsets. Can be repaired in sections

One piece

Often forged or cast. These tend to be stronger and more reliable.

Materials

Aluminium alloy is common, magnesium is light whilst composite structures have been tried. Need to be low in weight for un-sprung weight advantages but ridged enough to withstand loads.

Un-sprung

Sprung mass > define

Importance

7.2 Fitment

Centre lock

Offer quick and easy change from one set of wheels to another. Relies on one centre nut holding the wheel to the hub. Drive pegs are used to key the wheel to the hub. Retaining clips are utilised as a failsafe. NOTE: some cars use handed nuts on the LH and RH. Never fit retaining clip until wheels are torqued. Drive pegs are a good pre-check

Multi-bolt/stud fixing

The standard option. Wheel studs are easier to use than wheel bolts.

7.3 Inspection

Wheels should be inspected for:

- Leak down test (partially split rims) > puncture, valve leaking (seat, insert), between tyre and bead and rim, crack.
- Trueness
- Tightness of fasteners holding split rim together, condition of fixing nuts/bolts. Condition of drive pegs (male and female)
- DP crack testing can be carried out whilst other expensive NDT methods can be used such as CT X-ray
- NOTE: the weakest part of the rim is usually the inside (excluding accident damage) as it is furthest away from the centre.

Valves

- Stubby or motorcycle valves should be used to ensure the valve isn't proud of the tyre to avoid the risk of damaging the valve
- Caps should also be fitted to ensure debris cannot interfere
- A valve core key is a useful tool and should be used periodically to ensure tightness
- Valves are a serviceable item and should be replaced annually

Balancing

- Wheels should be balanced with clean wheels and tyres (pick up and tyre cleaning methods)
- Wheels weights should be taped with aluminium foil tape or similar
- Wheel balance should be checked before each event to alleviate symptoms

Knurling

- Bead knurling can be carried out to try and control or reduce the tyres from sipping on the rim when pressures are low.

Sizing

Very simple for race wheels

- 6"x10" means 6 inches wide with a diameter of 1o inches
- Rim shape is determined by a letter coding. 'J' is the most commonly used.

Offsets

- These determine how to wheel will sit on the car based on how far the centre of the wheel is from the back face of the mating wheel face.
- Zero - central to wheel, positive - outer edge of wheel, negative - further in than zero

Tyres pick up:

Dirt, debris, <u>discarded rubber</u> that adheres to the tyre surface when warm (raise of ground)

Tyre cleaning:

- Hot air gun and scraper (not good for longevity of the tyre, heating up will cause tyre to harden over time)
- Hard plastic brush
- Warm soapy water and rasp file (wood shaving tool)

Vertical load:

- Vehicle weight
- Aero
- Weight transfer

Mechanical grip:

- Geo
- Suspension set up

Un-sprung weight:

Weight that is not supported by the springs. Eg, wheels/tyres, brakes, uprights, etc. The lighter the better the contact between the tyre and the roads surface. Helps during bumps, undulations, transitions, etc. Faster reacting suspension (low inertia).

Sprung weight:

Weight supported by the springs. Eg chassis, driver, engine, gearbox, bodywork, etc. the heavier the sprung mass the stiffer the spring should be to keep the vehicle off of the ground.

8.0 Tyres

Why are tyres important:

- The only part of the car in contact with the ground
- All forces go through the tyres
- The car is only as good as the tyres performance and every component is designed to optimise their performance
- A valid and vital tuning tool
- We must have good knowledge and understanding of them in order to effectively tune out car

8.1 Key Design Principles

Passenger car - occupant comfort (NVH: noise, vibration and harshness)

Race car - optimise handling by ensuring tyre contact patch loadings with minimal variation

What do the tyres have to provide us with?

- Acceleration
- Braking
- Cornering
- Grip
- Ride and feel
- A combination of all of the above

- All of this comes from a selection of the right compound and construction - see Avon tyres motorsport website for compounds and patterns.

250/750R13   width in mm   diameter in mm   R=Radial tyres size in inches

The difference in compound is how long they've been baked in the oven for.

http://www.avonmotorsport.com/motorsport-tyres

Avon

Dunlop

Pirelli

Kuhmo

Michelin

Yokohama

Sizes:

- Radial - 230/7570R13
- Cross ply - 10.0/20.0.0-13

- Tyres width/tyres diameter/rim diameter

- Be aware of different manufactures taking measurements in different ways at different pressures, this can affect fitment, gearing and more.

Construction:

- Sidewall
- Shoulder - joins tread to side wall (most common to fail)
- Belts
- Bead
- Carcass   tie the rubber together - holds it all together
- Liner

Contact patch:

The contact patch is the area of the tyres that is in contact with the road, it is affected by the following factors:

- Vertical load - forces tyres into the ground
- Tyre pressure - changes the shape of the tyre
- Camber - affects which part of the tyre is on the track during different conditions

- Slip angle - effectively manipulates and scrubs the contact patch across the circuit

Why do the factors affect it:

Vertical load?

Tyre pressure?
Low pressure - soft sprung, increase damping
High pressure - stiff, decrease in damping

Camber?

Slip angle?

Slip ratio and slip angle:

Slip ratio (%) = ((vehicle speed - wheel speed) ÷ vehicle speed) × 100

Slip ratio is the difference between vehicle speed and wheel speed. Therefore, monitoring the difference or grip level during braking or accelerating.

Slip ratio (%) = ((100 - 100) ÷ 100) × 100 = 0%

Slip ratio (%) = ((100 - 105) ÷ 100) × 100 = -5% (acceleration)

Slip ratio (%) = ((105 - 100) ÷ 105) × 100 = 4.8% (braking lock up)

Slip ratio (%) = ((97 - 108) ÷ 97) × 100 = -11.3%

Slip ratio (%) = ((110 - 123) ÷ 110) × 100 = -11.8%

Slip ratio (%) = ((55 - 42) ÷ 55) × 100 = 23.6%

Vehicle speed = GPS

Wheel speed = wheel speed sensor

Cornering force vs slip angle with varying vertical load:

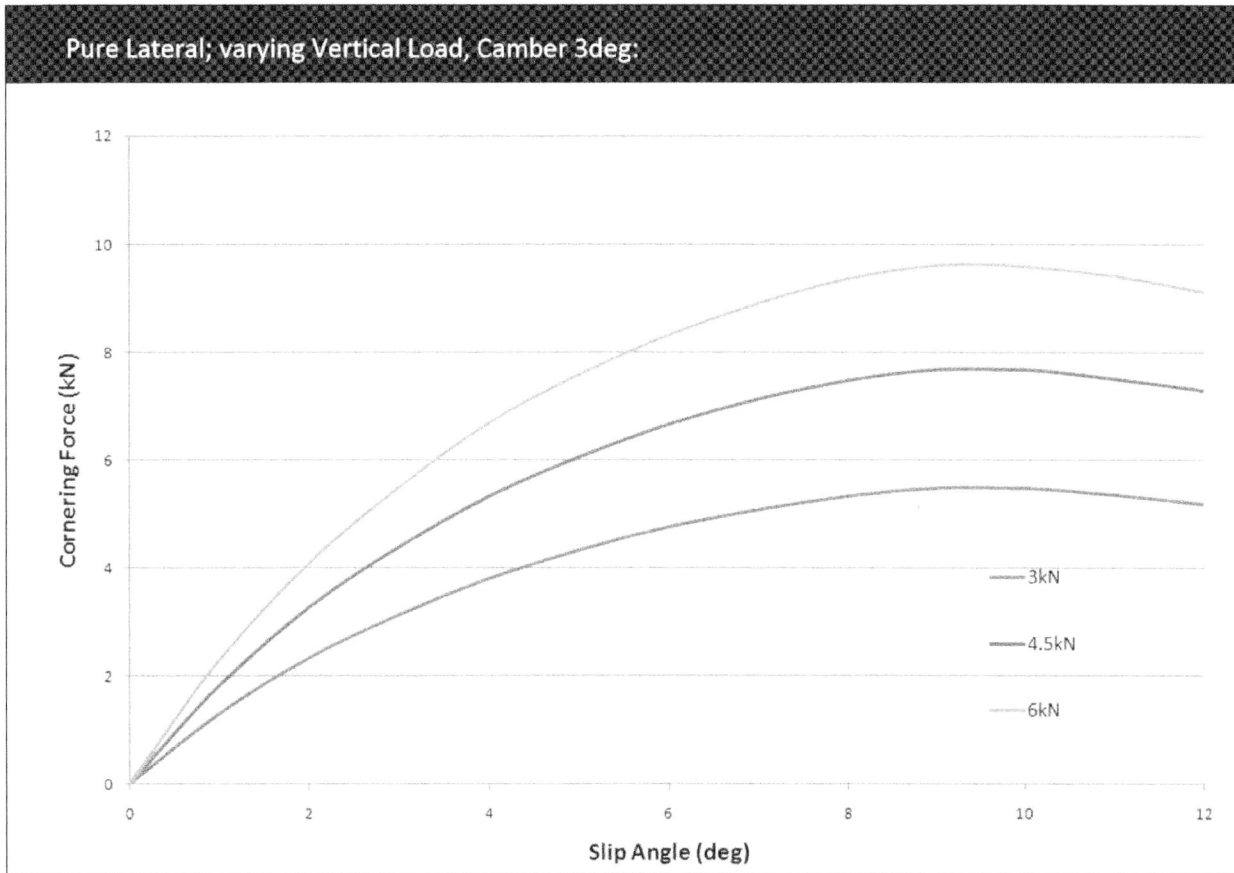

- A tyre must generate a slip angle to produce grip. There is an optimum window in which the tyres must perform within.
- Vertical load shows that the more we have, the more cornering force (grip) we produce.

Cornering force vs slip angle with varying camber:

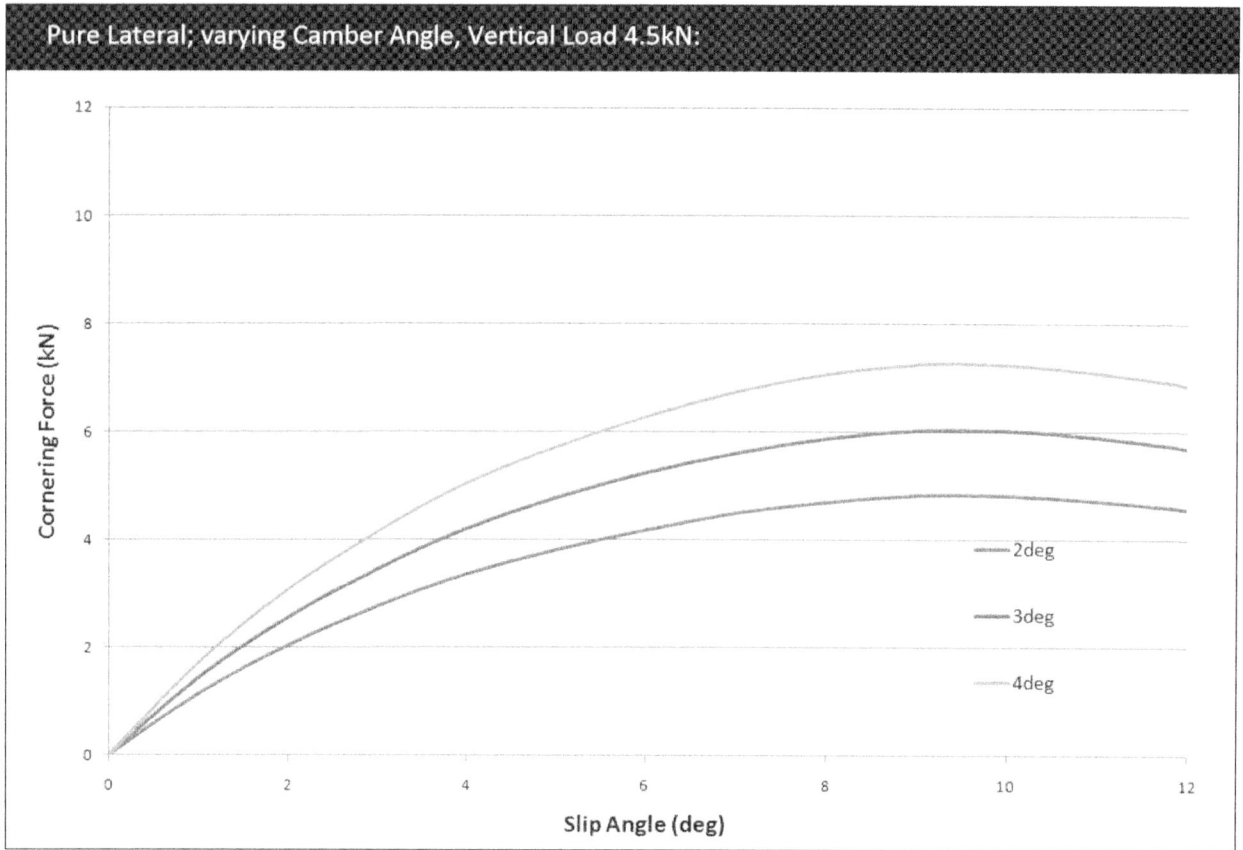

Pure Lateral; varying Camber Angle, Vertical Load 4.5kN:

Camber:

- Vertical load shows that the more we have, the more cornering force (grip) we reduce

Longitudinal force vs slip ratio with varying vertical load:

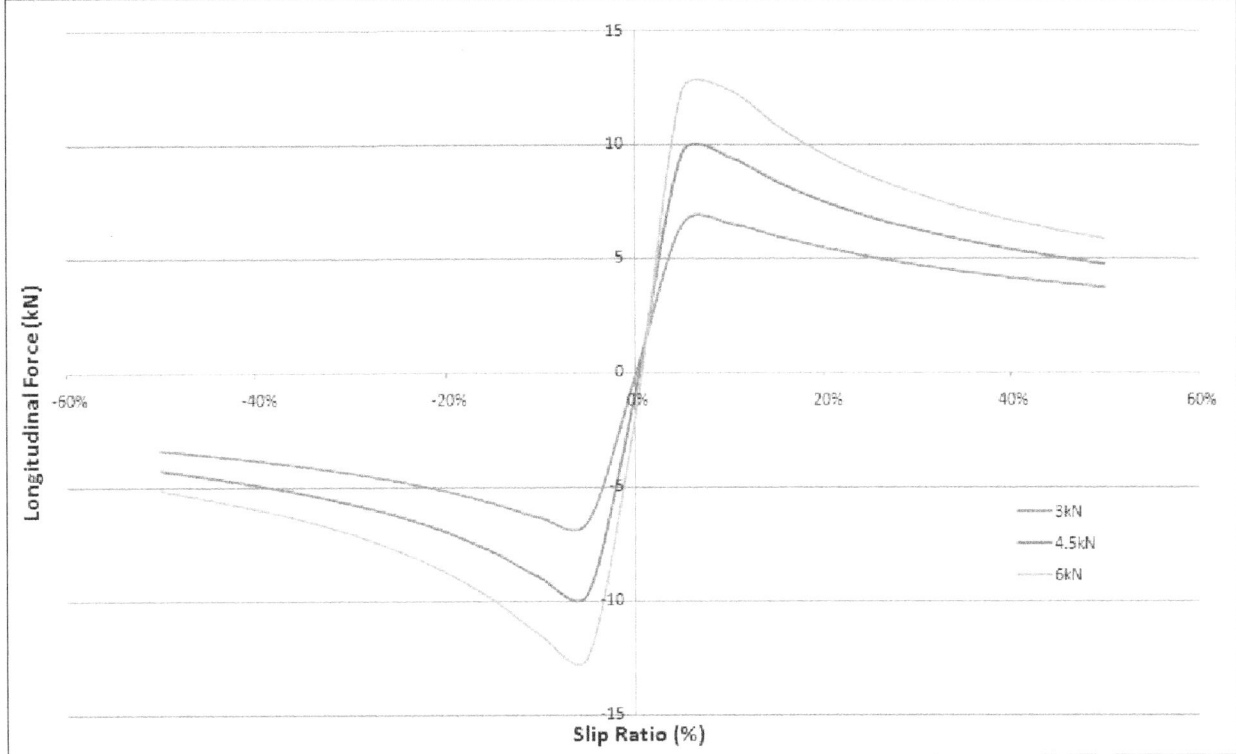

- Optimum slip ratio is between 5-8%
- Increase in vertical load will

Self-aligning torque vs slip angle with varying vertical load:

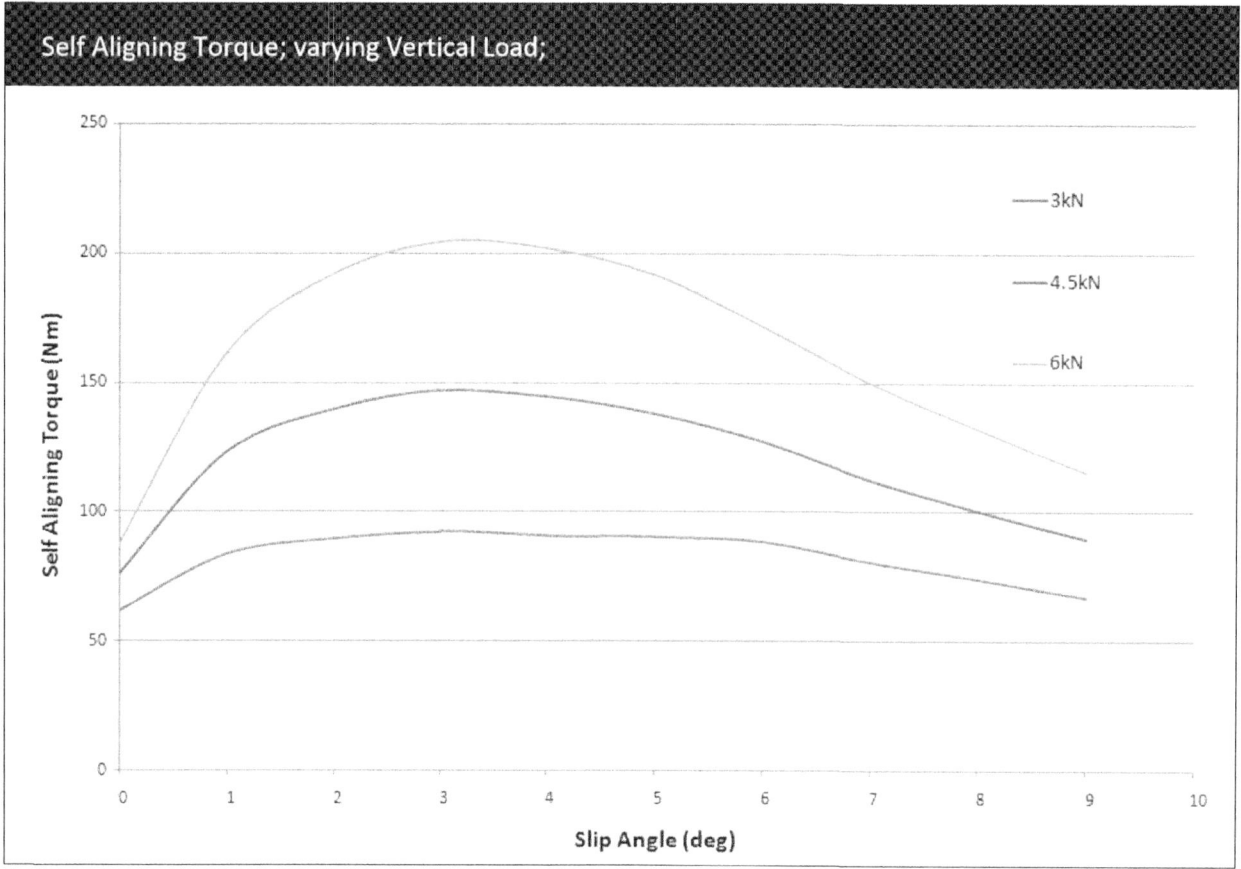

Self Aligning Torque; varying Vertical Load;

(Non-geometric) SAT - a tyres resistance to run away from centre

When peak of slip angle is exceeded, we lose grip - understeer/oversteer

Combined: The Grip Circle

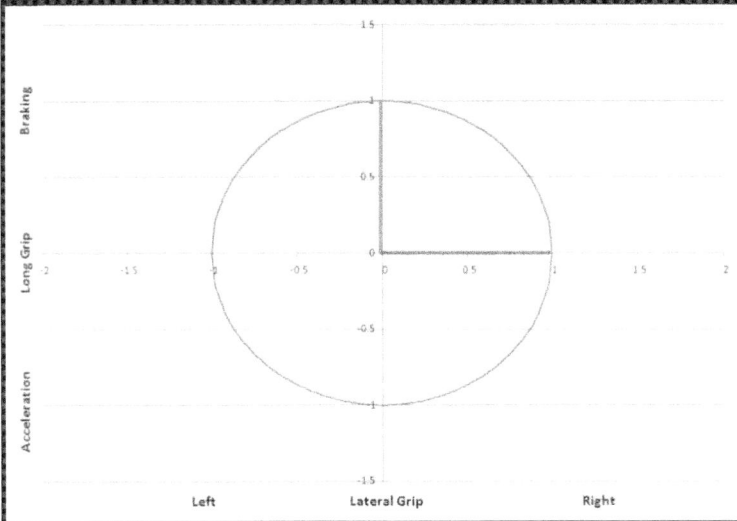

Case 1: Pure Lateral

Tyre can achieve Maximum Lateral Grip

Lateral = 1

Case 2: Pure Longitudinal

Tyre can achieve Maximum Longitudinal Grip

Longitudinal = 1

Combined: The Grip Circle

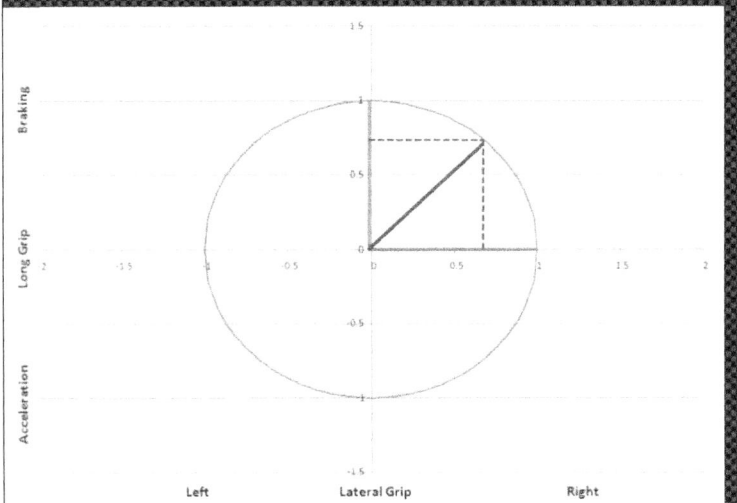

Case 3: Combined Grip

Tyre can not achieve Maximum Lateral Grip and Longitudinal Grip at the Same time

Lateral = 0.7

Longitudinal = 0.7

Therefore we can only develop 70% of our potential lat & long at the same time.

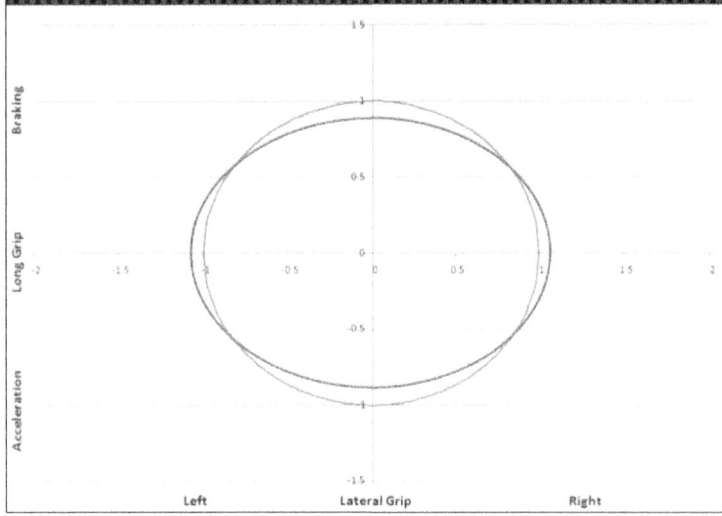

Grip Circle Comparison for Different Manufacturers

Comparison of Manufacturers:

——— Manufacturer "A"
Better Longitudinal Potential
Less Lateral Potential

——— Manufacturer "B"
Less Longitudinal Potential
Better Lateral Potential

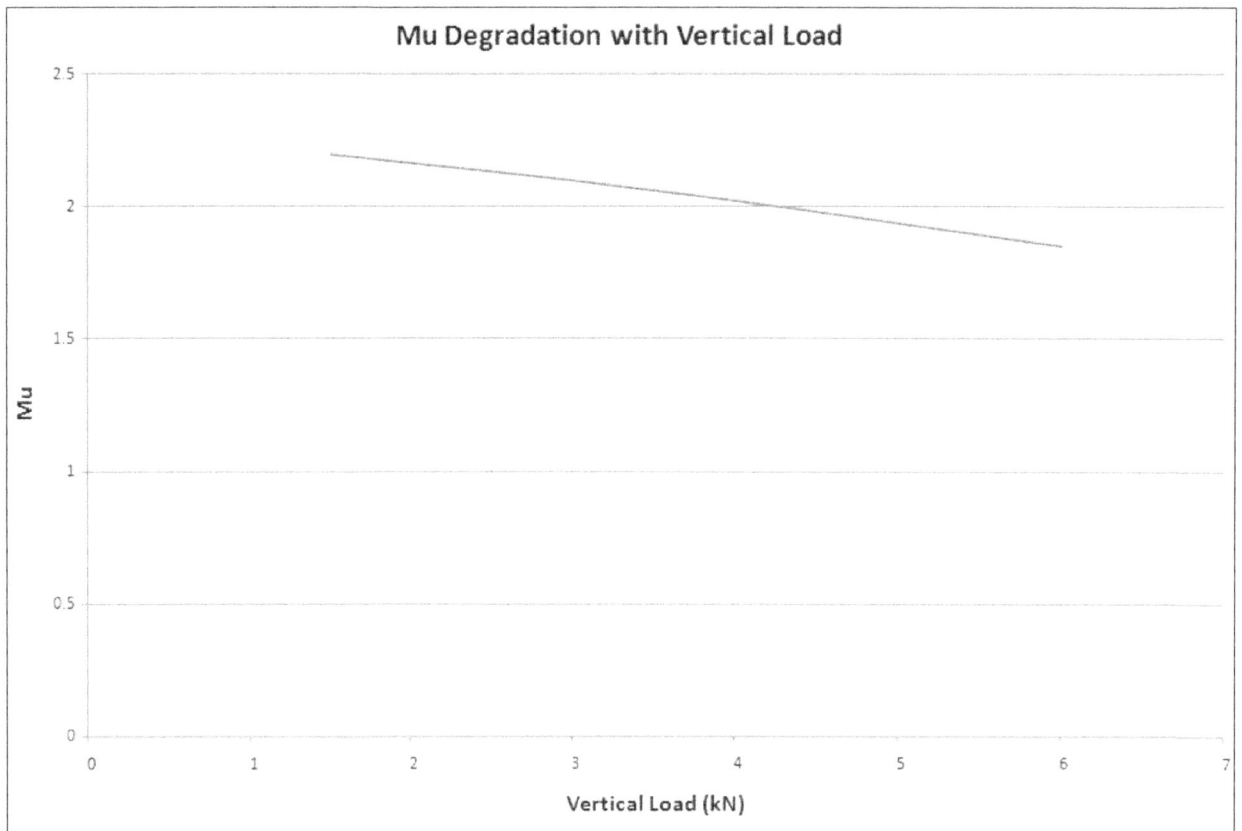

Mu Degradation with Vertical Load

8.2 Tyre Acting as a Damper & Spring

The tyre forms an important part of the spring and damping system of the suspension, particularly in control of the un-sprung mass. See Avon motorsport tyre website

Construction, side wall height and pressure have a large effect on their performance.

NOTE: very low pressure can cause damage to the tyre structure.

Tyre stiffness ratios: Going from Avon to a new tyre

Avon tyre vertical stiffness: Rear = 17.5 Front = 17 (Kg/mm)

$17 \div 17.5 = 0.97:1$

Bridgestone vertical stiffness: Rear = 16.7 Front = 14.4

$14.4 \div 16.7 = 0.86:1$ - make spring adjustments if chosen

Kumho vertical stiffness: Rear = 19.6 Front = 18.3

$18.3 \div 19.6 = 0.93:1$

Dunlop vertical stiffness: Rear = 21.6 Front = 15.8

$15.8 \div 21.6 = 0.73:1$

Yokohama vertical stiffness: Rear = 17.8 Front = 17

$17 \div 17.8 = 0.96:1$

8.2.1 Pressures

The tyre pressure determines the spring rate and contact patch of the tyre and we aim for a specific hot pressure when on track… we can only set them cold. As they are worked, the pressure increases.

1 bar = 14.7 psi

Radical PR6 target pressures 21-22psi and often start at cold around 16 rear and 17 front

Circuit tyre, surface, track temperature and other factors affect pressure increase

Ensure you gauge is calibrated. You can also log pressure

Pressures can also vary dependent upon what they are filled with, air from a pump or a compressor contains varying levels of moisture which is unstable and unpredictable.

Dry air (inert) such as nitrogen can be used to provide more stabilised and consistent pressure increases but this is done correctly, and tyres will need purging to ensure only nitrogen is present within the tyre.

8.2.2 Circuit Generation

A circuit can develop and change over the course of an event and the surface tyre varies from circuit to circuit.

Green - low grip, debris, dust, oils and fluids from rain shower, old rubber

Rubbered in - the circuit has a build-up of rubber impregnated on the racing line, providing good grip in dry, poor in wet. Dust and debris are also removed (marbles)

Surface tyre - aggregate and surface roughness (how much it's been compacted, high is better but will wear tyres quicker) - can affect grip and degradation levels - changes with circuit erosion and wear from environed and use.

8.2.3 Temperatures

- circuit/conditions etc...

Tyre temperatures should be monitored to compare the difference between front and rear axles and the spread across each tyre itself.

It can indicate car balance and any camber issues.

We can measure the temperature in 3 different ways-

1. Infra-red (IR) sensors - surface temperature
2. Pyrometer - bulk temperature (typically at 3mm)
3. Rim temperature sensor - indication of bulk temperature

Temperatures should be measured instantly

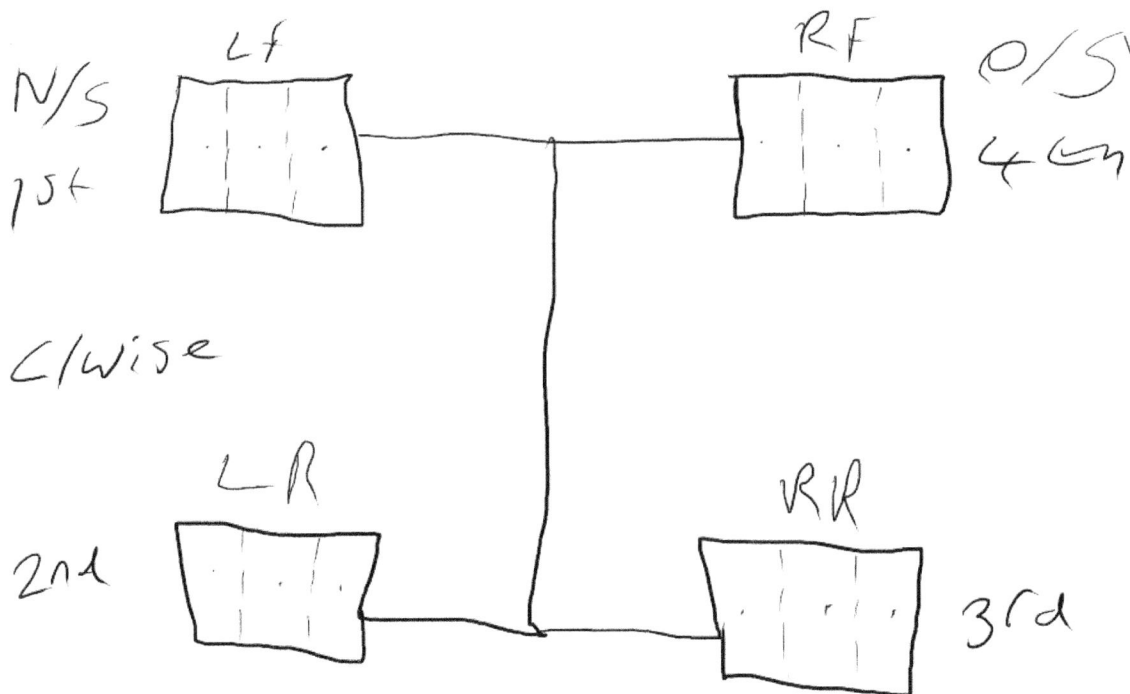

N/S
1st

Lf

RF

O/S
4cm

C/wise

2nd

LR

RR

3rd

- Variation across the tyre
- Balance between F + R

Temps too high will cause blistering and delamination.
Temps too low will cause graining and low drip levels.
Difference between surface and bulk must be minimal.

Graining is when the surface temp is higher than the temp inside the tyre.

Temps and pressures must be measured asap after a run starting with the most heavily loaded tyre first.

The inner edge of the tyre should be the hottest. Typical spreads are 10-15C at the front and 5-10C at the rear.

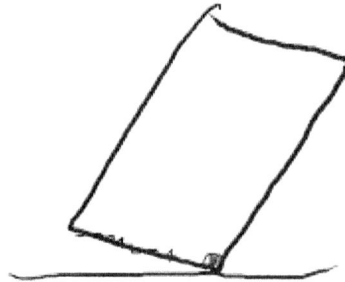

More camber at the front - rear traction

- LF corner entry to apex is heavily loaded

Degradation - normal tyre wear

Temp	Grip	Degradation
<60	Low	Low
65-70	Medium	Low
85-90	High	Medium
90-95	Very High	High
100+	Medium>Low	Very high

Temperatures
Outside>Middle>Inside

Outside	Middle	Inside
82	88	94
76	88	99
86	88	90
86	85	87
82	92	90

Front tyre average temp   Rear tyre average temp

100	90 - under
90	105 - over
70	90 - under
90	70
105	105
70	70

Generating heat:

3 main sources of temperature generation:

1. Environmental, brakes, (off car - tyre blankets, rim heaters, ovens)
2. Strain energy - generated by side wall and tread deflection
3. Friction energy - generated by the tyre slipping across the surface of the track

- Steering - the driver can stimulate front tyre temperature by weaving the car; forcing a lateral strain energy through the tyre. Front/rear temperature generation: 80%/20%
- Braking - braking stimulates tyre temperature by generating longitudinal slip at the tyre surface and by radiating heat from the brake system. Front/rear temperature generation: 55%-45% (mid-engine car)
- Acceleration - applying tractive load to the tyres will naturally increase tyre temperature. Caution should be taken by the driver not to be too aggressive on the throttle. Front/rear temperature generation: 15%-85%

Tyre blankets:
Ad: compact, tyres can be kept wrapped until last second
Dis: temperature generation at the tyre surface, surface curing

Tyre ovens:
Ad: even temperature build up
Dis: large, tyres need to be removed early > temp drop

Rim heaters:

Ad: compact, temperature spreads from bulk through to tyre surface

Dis: difficult to modulate the bulk and surface temperatures

Tyre durometer - shore hardness - tyre surface

Temperature effect on tyres

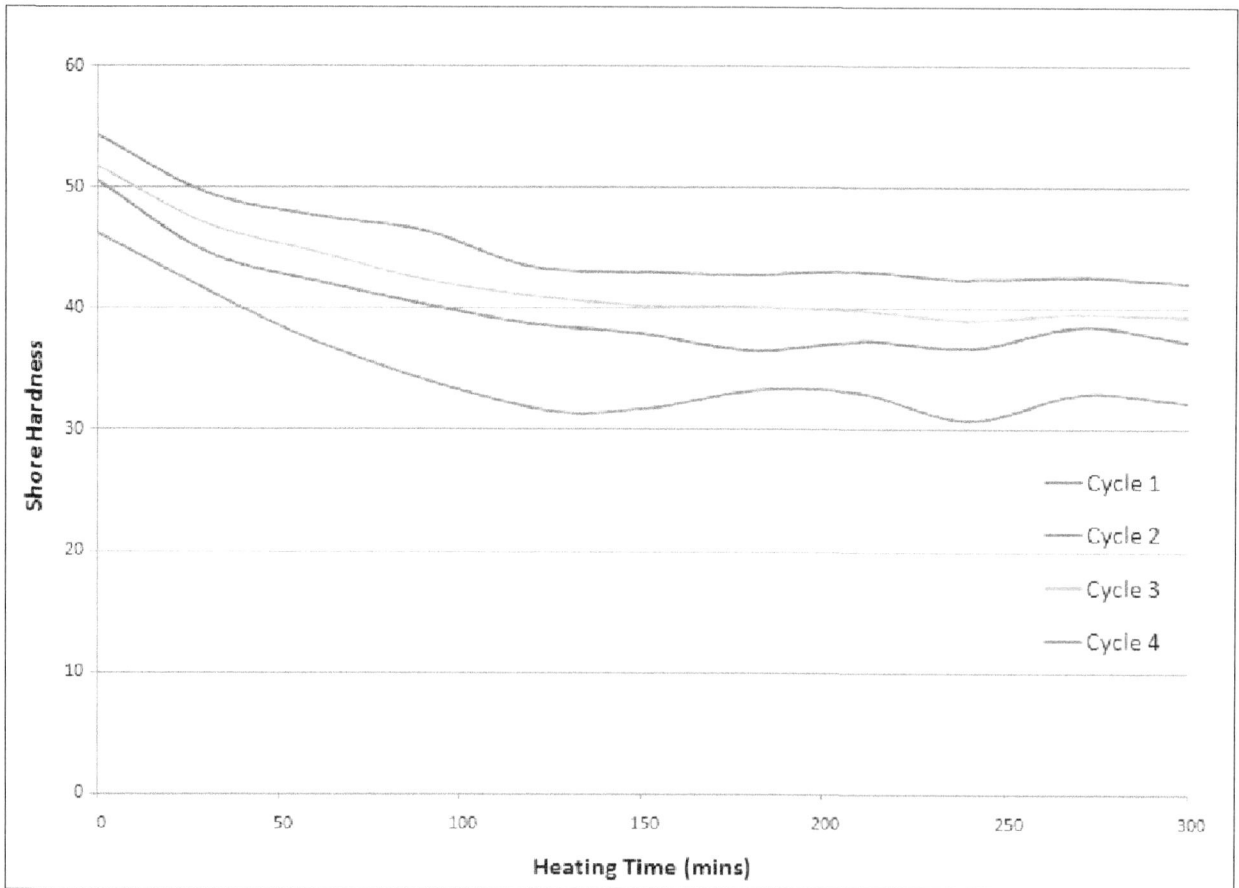

Heat cycle - use at temperature for a period of time before cooling

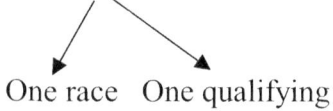

One race   One qualifying

Hardness vs temp/heat cycle

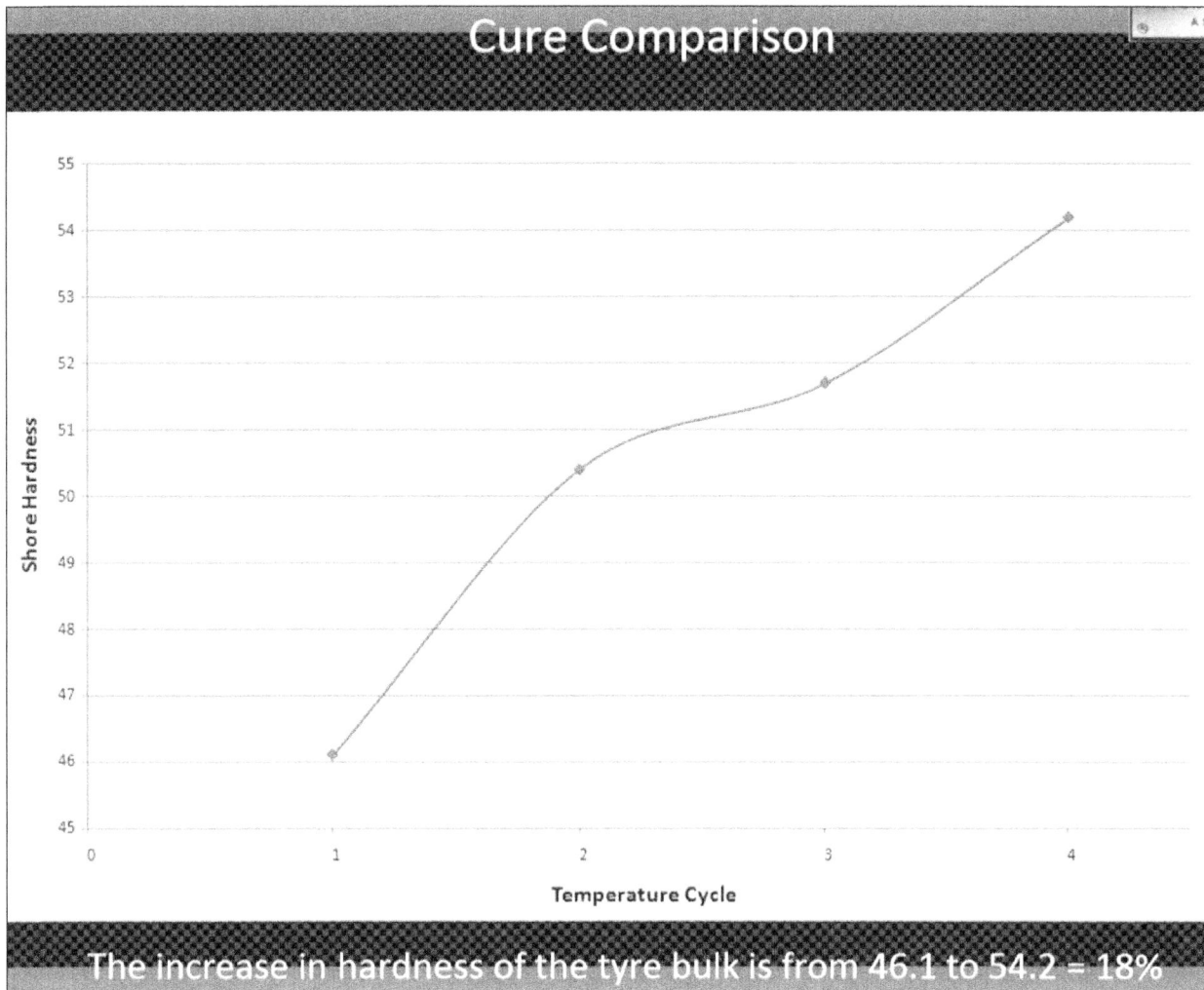

Cure Comparison

The increase in hardness of the tyre bulk is from 46.1 to 54.2 = 18%

8.2.4 Tyre Defects

- Graining - shear failure of the tyre caused by a temperature difference between surface and bulk. Caused by tyre compound too soft, driver pushing too hard when the tyres aren't at the right operating temp or when the track and ambient temps are very low. Tyre can come back you afterwards depending upon how they are treaded

- Delamination - tyre tread separates from the carcass. Under inflation, overloading and excessive heat are the main causes. A cause an immediate blowout or flailing parts - leading to damage and risk of accident

- Blistering - caused from overheating a certain area of the tyre - inner edge or from a lock up. Tyre is softened and rubber is scrubbed off of the tyre after the blister has occurred

- Degradation - general tyre wear based on compound, track surface, temperature and vertical loadings

Tyre markings:

Tyres should be marked to identify themselves. You can include position, car/driver, set number and direction arrows

Wear indicators:

Wet tyres often don't have markings for tread depth
Slicks do have them
Moulded and hand cut

Storage and breaking/scrubbing in:

Tyres are susceptible to temperature and UV light so should be stored at room temp in the dark and ideally wrapped in tyre bags, black film or bin liners.
When produced, tyres have release agent applied so that they can be released from the mould. This waxy layer is slippery and must be removed before pushing hard in the car. After this is a gentle warming up cycle is used to roughen the surface of the tyre to increase grip and longevity throughout its use.

Cross ply and radial tyres:

Cross ply has a harder side wall
More camber on a radial tyres because of the side wall flex

Radial   Cross

-3.5	-3.0		-1.0	-0.8
-2.5	-2.0		-0.5	-0.3

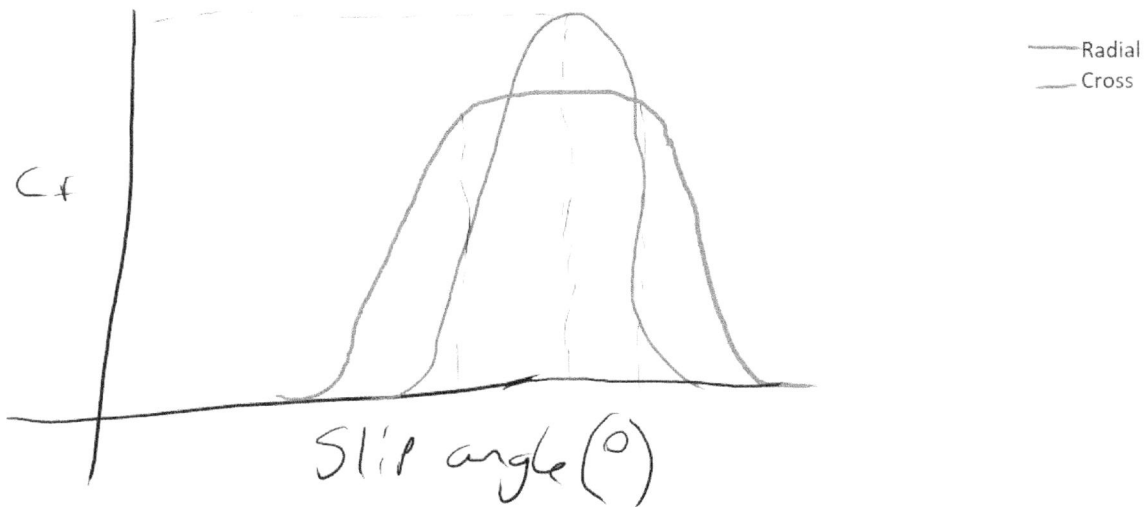

Radial
Cross

C_f

Slip angle (°)

Radial offers more grip but are peakier.

Cross plies offer less peak grip but provide maximum grip over a larger slip angle

Camber is often significantly reduced for cross ply tyres. Eg, 3.5 degrees for radical front to 1 degree for cross fronts.

Car balance theories:

In fast corners aerodynamics (ride heights and wing settings) have more influence on the balance than in slower corners.

In mid and slow speed corners the weight distribution and diff settings are most important.

Tune the dampers to the springs, not the springs to the dampers.

Always pay attention to reach the correct tyre temperatures. No car can reach its limit on too cold tyres. No car can be reasonably balanced with a significant difference between front and rear tyre temperatures.

Run the car always as low as possible, although without going too stiff on springs or composing geo.

9.0 Chassis

9.1 Set up

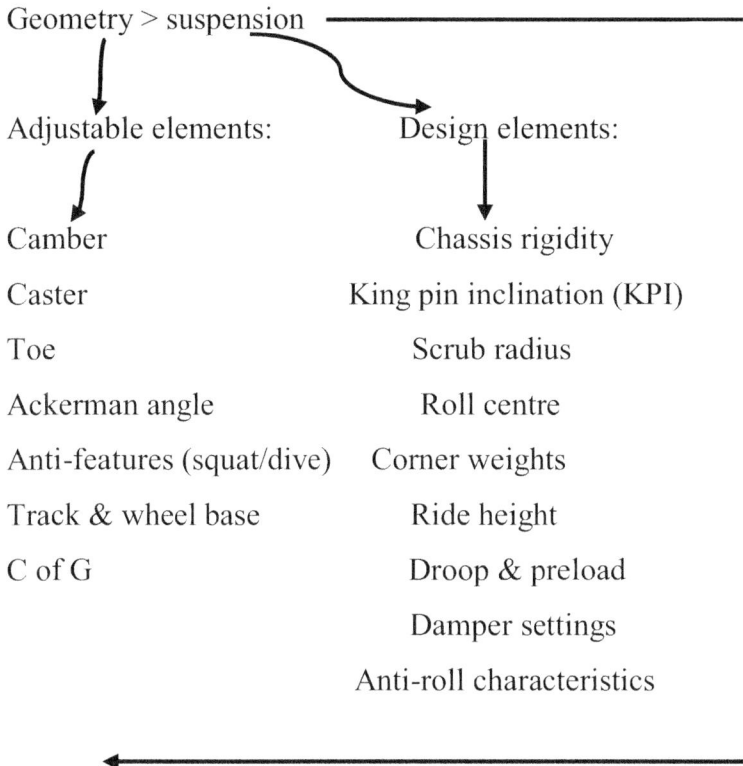

Geometry > suspension

Adjustable elements: Design elements:

Camber   Chassis rigidity

Caster   King pin inclination (KPI)

Toe   Scrub radius

Ackerman angle   Roll centre

Anti-features (squat/dive)   Corner weights

Track & wheel base   Ride height

C of G   Droop & preload

                                  Damper settings

                               Anti-roll characteristics

1. <u>Race ready</u> ⟶ Tyre pressures (hot)

Driver or driver weight (and co-driver)

Fluid levels > 1/2 race fuel

Ballast

Bodywork for final check

Correct wheels & tyres > set up wheels

2. <u>Flat floor</u> before set up is carried out (flat & level)

3. <u>Check all components</u> are fit for purpose

  > Wheel torques, bearing & rod end play and general steering & suspension condition

4. What is adjustable? What is it set to? What does the customer want? Feedback?

  > Kit

5.<u>Prepare car</u> for set up?   Tyre pressures

Removal of anti-roll bar

Fully soften dampers (count clicks & record)

6.Put onto <u>flat patch</u> > settle the car

7.Ride height/drop height/ground clearance

> lowest pint of car to the floor (regulation)

Different levels in front and rear ride height is rake > downforce floor - Venturi > shift in aero balance forwards

> geometric/chassis set up value > defined by point on the chassis

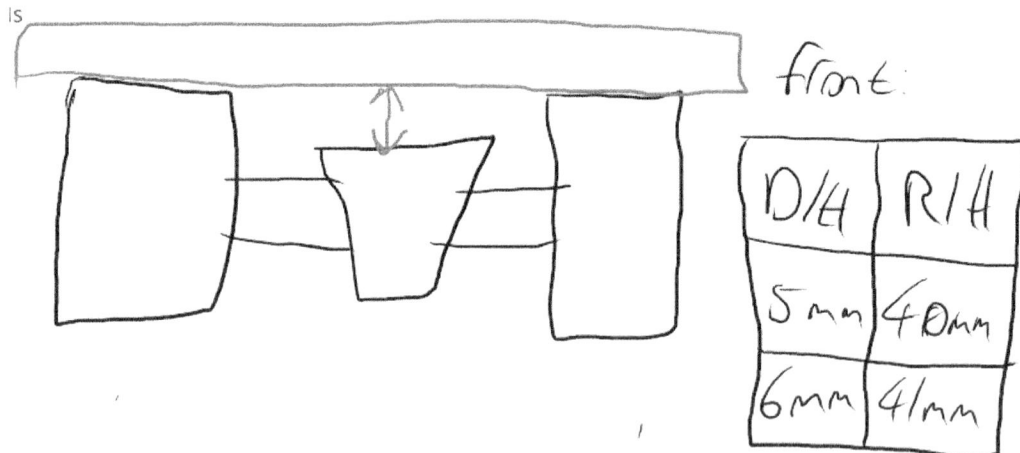

front:	
D/H	R/H
5 mm	40 mm
6 mm	4/mm

8.Caster angle (degrees)

> stability > self-centring

> always positive

> dynamic camber change > gives negative camber on the outside wheel

> positive on the inside wheel

> even on both sides > 4 - 8 degrees

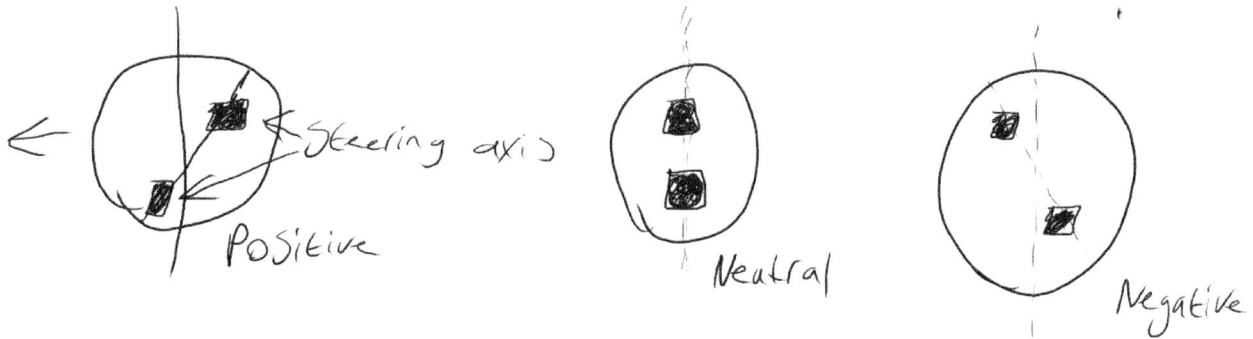

Positive — Steering axis — Neutral — Negative

9.Camber (degrees)

   > negative

   > unequal > circuit direction, circuit characteristics, determined by tyre temperatures

           > front to back

   > -2 to -4 degrees (radial)

   > 0.5 to - 1 (cross ply)

   > <-5 (tin tops)

Negative:

-3-4 degrees front

-2-3 degrees rear

10.Toe/tracking/geometry

↳Not sensitive to uneven floors

Units of measurement - mm, fractions of an inch, degrees)decimal), degrees, minutes & seconds

   • Start with rear axle

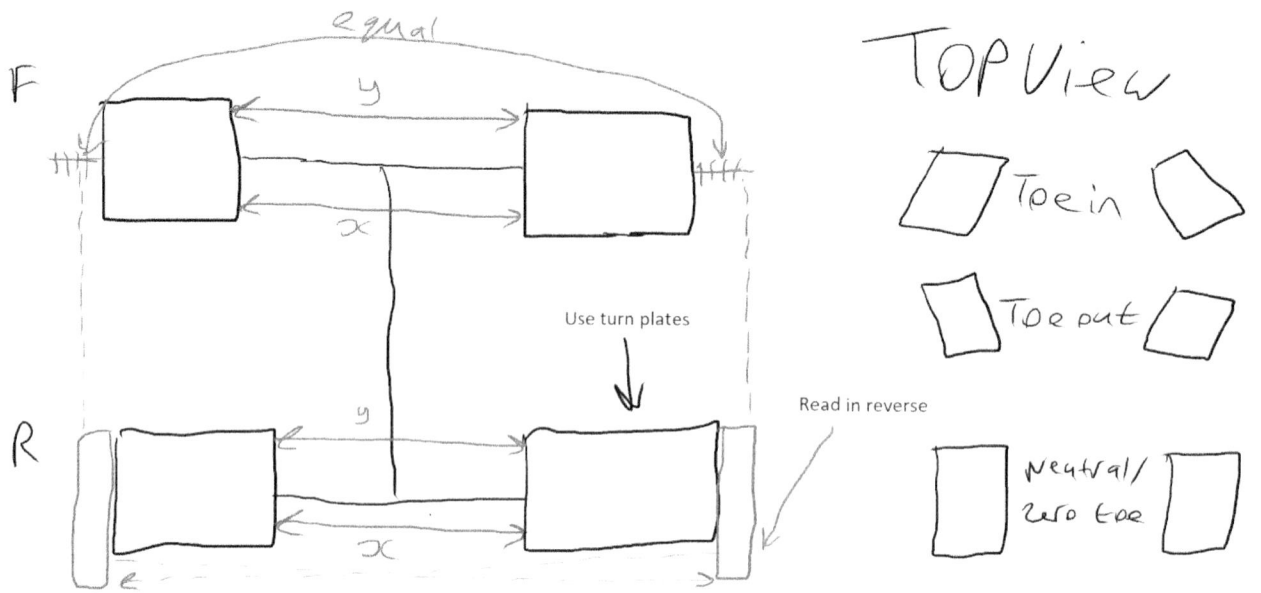

F — equal — y — x

Use turn plates

Read in reverse

R — y — x — e

TOP View

Toe in

Toe out

Neutral/
zero toe

If the rear axle doesn't track the front wheel then we have a thrust angle & line

If an adjustment is made to caster or camber you will directly affect toe. That's why its left until last.

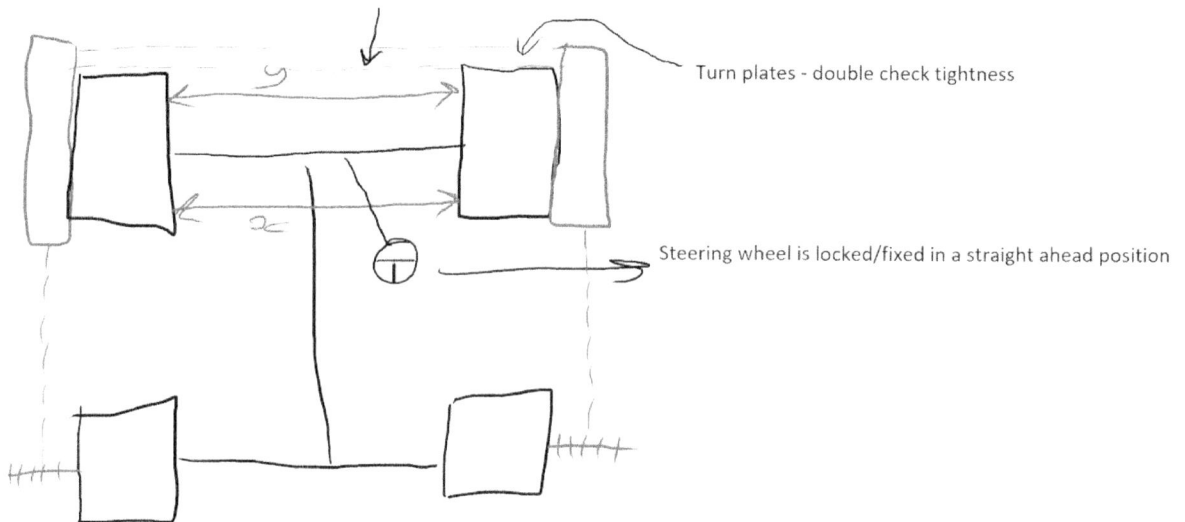

y — x

Turn plates - double check tightness

Steering wheel is locked/fixed in a straight ahead position

Toe out Toe in   Toe out   Toe in
6543210123456   6543210123456

1mm of toe out across axle
4mm toe in across the axle

Toe in - stable condition - stability as the wheels are pushing forward into the centre - scrub/heat generation - additional rolling resistance (toe out does same)

Front steered, rear driven

F - Toe in or <u>out</u> (allows good initial turn in - but becomes to dart, tendency to wander, reacts to bumps and undulations) (1mm out - 2mm out)

R - Toe in

Front steered, front driven

F - Toe in or toe out (driver preference like rear drive)

R - Toe in - toe out (allows rear to rotate & help steer in understeer situations)

0-3mm across axle

Radical = F - 1-2mm toe out

    R - 2-3mm toe in

11.Corner weights

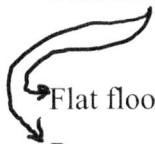

Flat floor sensitive

Race ready

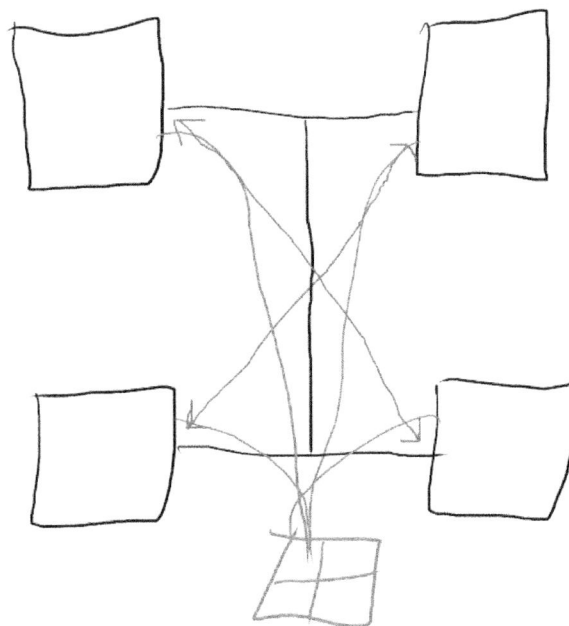

Measures:

- Cross weight - diagonal measurement
- L:R weight distribution (design and build phase) (single seater/sports prototype = 50:50) (60:40)
- R:R weight distribution (design and build phase) (45:55) (60:40)
- Total weight - minimum weight - zero litres

Cross weight:

LF + RR = RF + LR

Even cross weight (50:50 (0.5-1%)) to ensure even handling between left- and right-handed corners (chassis balance) - adjustment made via ride height. Light cross weight has RH up, heavy cross weight has RH down - recheck ride height, rake & camber.

- Reset dampers
- Reset anti-roll bars
- Reset tyre pressures
- Double check all adjustable items for correct torque setting (driver ballast, fuel, tyres, bodywork refit)

10.0 Weight

Power to weight ratio: BHP/tonne

$$\text{Power (hp)} / \text{Weight (kg)} \times 1000 = \text{BHP/tonne}$$

$$250 / 500 \times 1000 = 400 \text{ BHP/tonne}$$

$$450 / 1400 \times 1000 = 321 \text{ BHP/tonne}$$

Weight:

- Stop it
- Accelerate it } least amount of weight the better
- Corner with it

4 x evenly loaded perform significantly better than 2 heavily loaded - 2 lightly loaded tyres

Weight transfer - lateral, longitudinal, diagonal (moving/dynamic)

$$\text{Long weight transfer} = \frac{\text{Accel (g)} \times \text{weight (lbs)} \times \text{CG height (inches)}}{\text{Track / Wheelbase (inches)}}$$

Lateral weight transfer

Centre of gravity - point at which all forces act from/through

- Balance/central point of all mass
- Position in a plan view
- Height

Centroid of mass axis (side view):

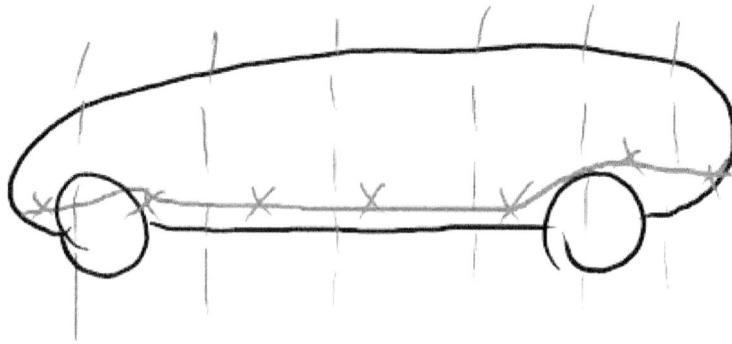

CG sits across the car

1G

1000 lbs

15"

Track: 64"

Wheelbase: 100"

$1 \times 1000 \times 15 / 100 = 150\text{lbs}$

$1 \times 1000 \times 15 / 64 = 234\text{lbs}$

$1.2 \times 1000 \times 15 / 100 = 180\text{lbs}$

$1.2 \times 1000 \times 15 / 64 = 281\text{lbs}$

$0.8 \times 1000 \times 15 / 100 = 120\text{lbs}$

$0.8 \times 1000 \times 15 / 64 = 187\text{lbs}$

$1 \times 1200 \times 15 / 100 = 180\text{lbs}$

$1 \times 1200 \times 15 / 64 = 281\text{lbs}$

$1 \times 800 \times 15 / 100 = 120\text{lbs}$

$$1 \times 800 \times 16 / 64 = 187\text{lbs}$$

$$1 \times 1000 \times 16 / 100 = 160\text{lbs}$$

$$1 \times 1000 \times 16 / 63 = 250\text{lbs}$$

Reduces weight transfer

Reduce weight (strength & fatigue)

Reduce CG height

Increase Wheelbase or Track

Track:

*Stability & reduction in weight transfer

Manoeuvrability, increase front area, increase weight

*Wheelbase - high speed stability

*Increased under floor aero advantage

Weight distribution (static)

- Build and design phase - CG location (Plan)

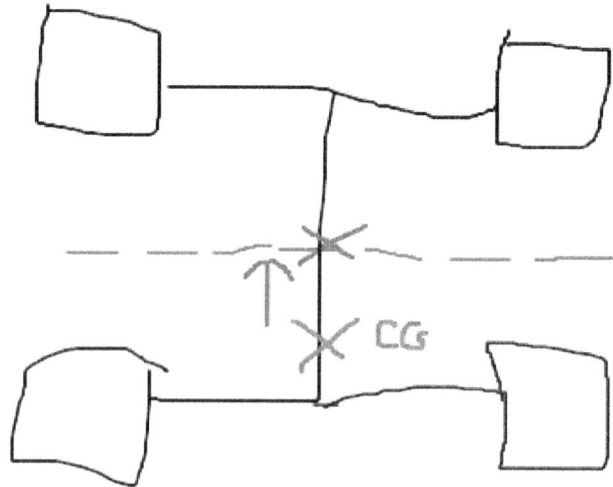

Rearward weight distribution > rear traction - acceleration - rearwards

> braking forces - shift in WT forwards that ends just in front of the centre line allowing rear brakes and tyres to be worked relativity hard

10.1 Weight Distribution

Focused on during the design and build phase. Weight distribution has a direct effect on cars handling and control response. In a perfect scenario all components will merge with out CG.

1. Driver
2. Engine
3. Gearbox & drivetrain
4. Fuel tank

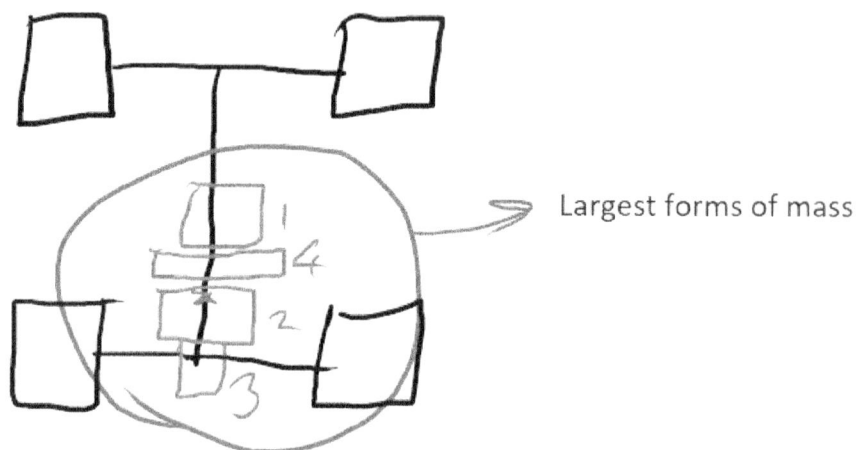

Largest forms of mass

Lat, long, diagonally - CG above ground level - WT will always occur - WT due to CG

- WT due to pitch and roll

movements

- Height and plan position

As low as possible

Left : Right - WD 50/50

Front : Rear - 45/55 or 40/60

Usually at the front of the engine

10.2 Polar Moment of Inertia

Inertia

A components reluctance to change direction or speed - rolling or rotating:

- Wheels
- Flywheel and clutch
- Drive/prop shafts
- Gears, diff
- Engine rotating and reciprocating mass

Polar moment of inertia:

The effects of mass placed outside of a cars track and wheelbase. It can produce a pendulum affect as seen in the drawing below.

Sizes, thicknesses and materials - reducing diameter helps the change of direction.

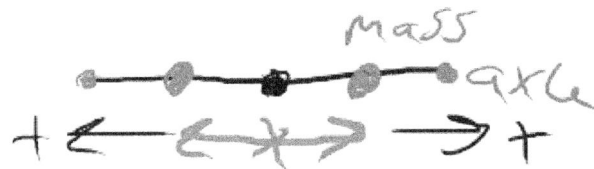

Any mass placed away from the CG will attempt to rotate around this point.

11.0 Suspension Development

Suspension development in Double Wishbone set ups

Outboard:

+ Ease of placement

+ Simple

+ Keeps damper cool (oil)

-High unsprung weight

-Detrimental to airflow

-Mass isn't central

-Doesn't allow adjustment in preload and ride hide

-Difficult to alter motion ratio

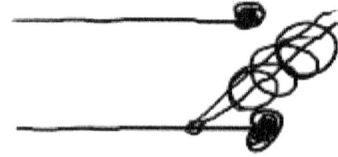

Inboard - Rocker arm:

+ Out of airflow

+ Central mass

+ Low unsprung

+ Ability in design to select our motion ratio

-Out of airflow - mono-tube gas filled

-Small weight increase

-Small raise in CG

Push/pull rod:

+ Acceptable airflow intrusion

+ Motion ratio design freedom

+ Ride height + preload independence

-More complex system

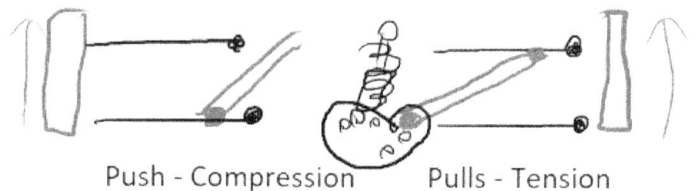

Push - Compression   Pulls - Tension

Monoshock:

+ Weight

+ Space and packaging

+ Roll and pitch rates are entirely separate

+ Roll rate infinitely tuneable

-Never seen on a rear of a car

Preload - is an upwards force when the spring is under tension using 'zero droop'

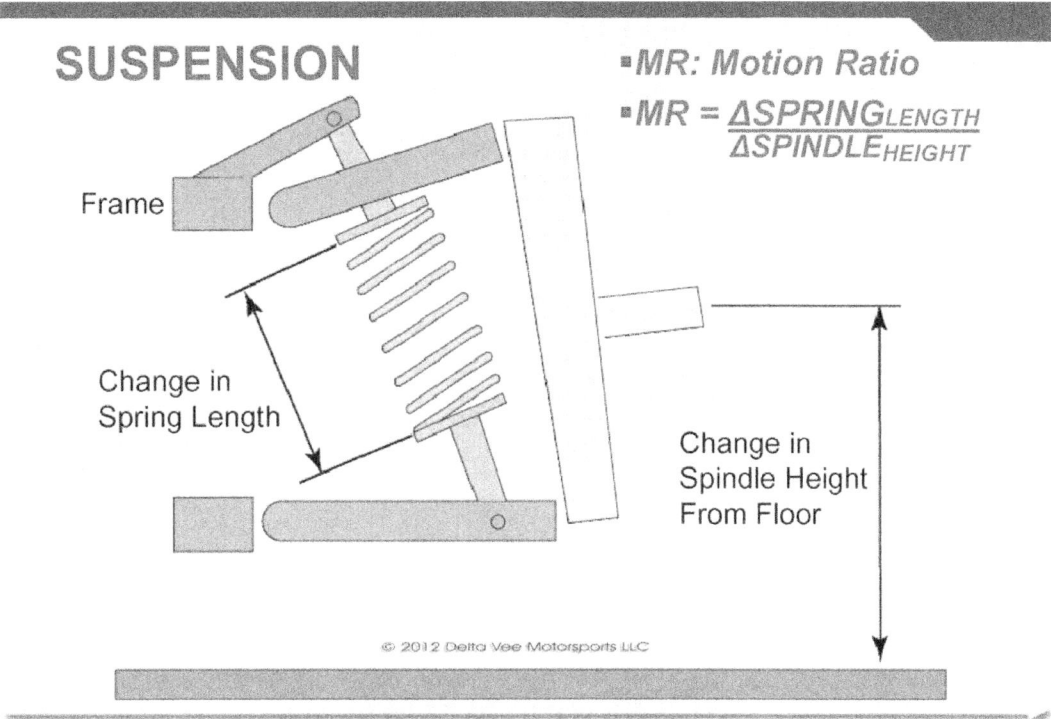

SUSPENSION

- MR: Motion Ratio
- $MR = \dfrac{\Delta SPRING_{LENGTH}}{\Delta SPINDLE_{HEIGHT}}$

Frame

Change in Spring Length

Change in Spindle Height From Floor

© 2012 Delta Vee Motorsports LLC

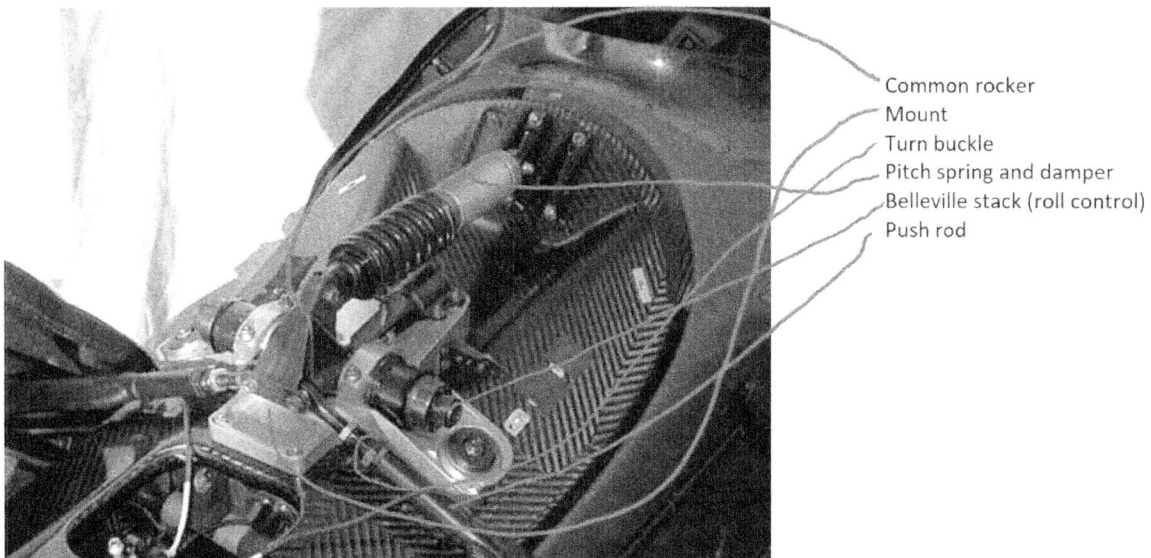

Common rocker
Mount
Turn buckle
Pitch spring and damper
Belleville stack (roll control)
Push rod

Anti-heave devices/3rd element - just a spring, just a damper, combination of the two, bump rubber stack (controls ride height with aero vertical load)

11.1 Anti Roll Bar Types

- Tee bar - most common
- N/U bar
- Nik-link
- Blade ARB

12.0 KPI/SAI/Scrub

KPI - King pin inclination } same thing
SAI - Steering axis inclination

Kingpin (steering axis) inclination and scrub radius/offset.

KPI is the angle of a drawn line between the top and bottom ball joint compared to the true vertical. KPI provides us with camber change, self-centring steering and is a factor of scrub radius/offset.

Always seen from front view. Line that intersects our steering axis i.e. top and bottom ball joint. Not camber. Done in the design phase.

KPI is generally fixed but is altered slightly on most systems when camber is changed. Packaging of a modern race car is a very difficult task and a number of compromises must be made to accommodate optimum suspension geometry, ample brake systems, hubs, etc.

KPI provides us with camber change and self-centring steering and is a factor of scrub radius/offset. As the steering axis rotates the wheel is pushed down into the ground (and jacking (lifting the car up)) and at the same time produces a reduction in negative camber.

- Reduction in camber
- Self-centring from pushing the wheel down

Zero KPI leads to a large amount scrub offset. What this means is that the turning centre of the steering axis is a long way from the centre of the tyre.

Included Angle = KPI + Camber
15+(-3)=12 degrees

Dragged around the outside of the rotation causing additional friction, wear and heavier steering. Large scrub offset/radius.

Camber

Positive KPI

Scrub radius

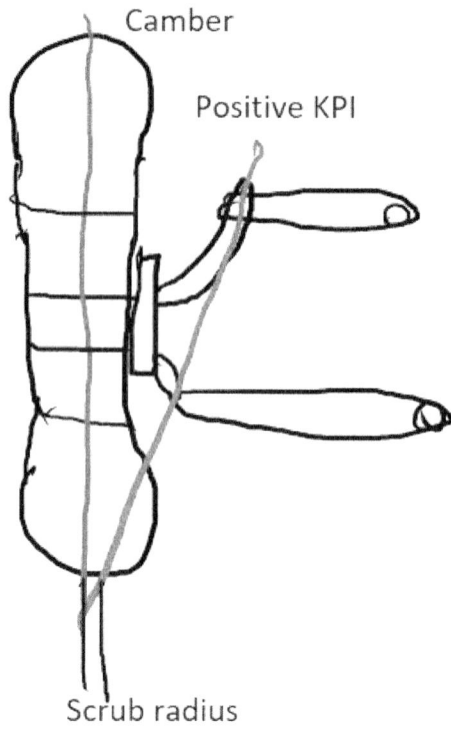

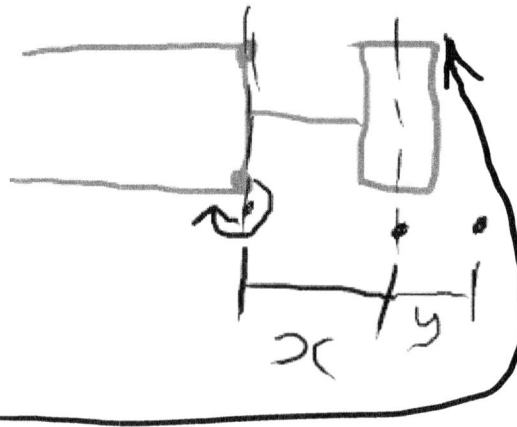

Large scrub offset/radius

0 scrub radius: Intersects at ground level

Positive scrub radius: Intersect below ground level

Negative scrub radius: Intersect above ground level

Scrub radius is the distance between the tyre centreline at ground level and SAI where is intersects the ground. An offset means that the tyre does not turn on its centreline, creating more friction and requiring more effort to turn.

13.0 Rear Suspension

- Beam/live axle - Mumford, Wobb, Panhard, Watts, 4-link (FWD)
- Live axle (RWD)
- Swing axle (don't need to talk about in assignment)
- De-Dion - has a beam but diff is attached to chassis (non-ind and ind)
- Trailing, Semi-trailing arm
- Double wishbone

A good website to look at is: http://www.susprog.com/

Non-Independent

+

- Lower in mass
- Fitment and location are easier

-

- Higher un-sprung mass
- One contact patch is affected by opposing side
- Limited adjustability

Independent

Layouts of rear suspension were also briefly mentioned in Section 2.0 of the book.

14.0 Motion Ratio & Wheel Rates

The difference between wheel rate and spring rate is vast, you will set your car up with a specific stiffness of spring but what is felt at the wheels is very different. Wheel rate takes the geometry of the suspension into the equation (motion ratio) and makes it easy to compare different cars. The leverage (motion ratio) dictates how strong the spring is at the wheels.

MR (Motion Ratio) - Is the relationship between a system that involves linkages whereby there is a difference in displacement between one end of a pivot and the opposing side.

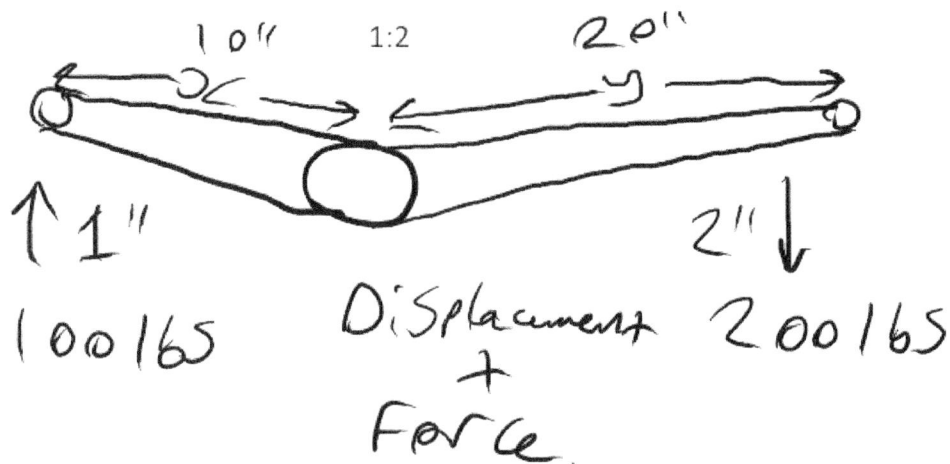

The drawing above shows wheel travel & damper travel. Altering the spring rate to provide a different rate at the wheels.

Motion ration = Wheel Travel ÷ Spring Travel

Wheel Rate = Spring Rate ÷ Motion Ratio^2

Motion ratio is not always linear.

MR = 1 ÷ 0.8 = 1.25:1

WR = 425 ÷ 1.25^2 = 272 lbs/inch

Other methods to calculate:

$MR = D1 \div D2$

$MR = D3 \div D4$

Angle Correction Factor

$(ACF) = Cosine A$

$WR = (MR)^2(C)(ACF)$

$C = Spring\ Rate$

MR can be adjusted on some cars.

$MR = 1 \div 0.95 = 1.05:1$

$WR = 425 \div 1.05^2 = 385\ lbs/inch$

Increasing + Decreasing wheel rate

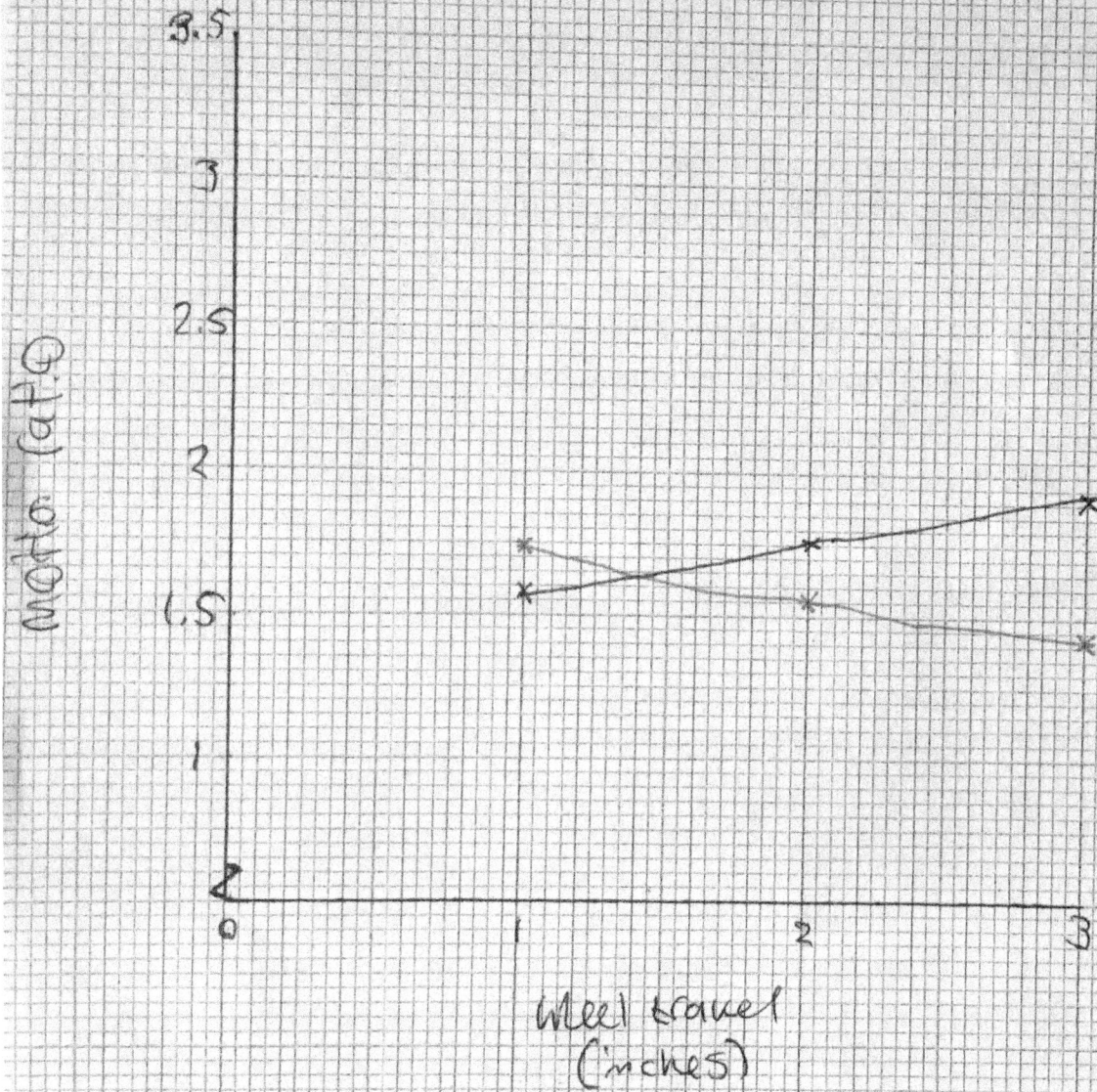

Increasing wheel rate
Decreasing wheel rate

15.0 Springs

Springs come in a variety shapes and sizes. They all perform the same duty in a suspension system. High end manufactures include Eibach and HyperCo whilst the budget end is Faulkner.

To support the sprung mass of the car.

Manufacturing tolerances to give a like to like comparison. High end batches will have closer tolerances than cheaper. Lighter (stronger material therefore needs less) and less sag.

Soft - More roll/pitch of sprung mass, follow the road pattern/contours.
Hard - More response, harsher ride, more variable contact patch loading (makes tyre work harder).

Inches to MM - Times inches by 25.4 = mm

MM to inches - divide mm by 25.4 = inches

LBS/inches to KG/mm - divide LBS by 56 = KG/mm

KG/mm to LBS/inches - times KG/mm by 56 = LBS/inches

Lbs/inches to N/mm - divide LBS by 5.7 = N/mm

N/mm to Lbs/inches - times by N/mm by 5.7 = Lbs/inches

Example:
200 lbs/inch=

N/mm = 200÷5.7=35 N/mm

KG/mm = 200÷56=3.6 or 3-4 KG/mm

1"

200lbs

2"

400lbs

3"

600lbs

4"

800lbs

etc

Radical:

Front - 325 lbs/inch

Rear - 400 lbs/inch   Stiffen the axle with more grip, soften axle with less grip.

There are 4 types of coil spring available:

Main, Tender, Helper, Progressive.

All springs will have ground and closed ends at either end.

Main with a tender. Main and helper. Main, tender and helper. Progressive with main & tender.

Main and progressive springs are made out of sprung round bar.

Tender and helper and made out of sprung flat bar.

Different types of mains are - linear, dual rate and progressive (starts narrow and gets gradually wider).

Tender springs:

A tender spring needs to be run in conjunction with a main spring in series and provides a softer initial rate when both springs are compressed together.

Once the tender spring has completely closed the spring rate becomes that of the main spring alone.

Tender springs are available in a range of linear and progressive spring rates.

Helper springs:
Helper springs are used to prevent the main spring from becoming loose (dislocated) in the spring seat when the wheel is in full droop.

Helper springs have a very low spring rate and therefore do not affect the suspension characteristics.

Typically, up to 50mm can be covered by a helper.

Thrust bearings to help the spring move freely while in use.

Spring joiners - keeps springs in line

Springs can be run like a series or in parallel
Parallel - 2 dampers = 1/2 the load, twice the oil (larger cooling capacity), fail safe if one breaks.
Spring rate 1 + spring rate 2 = overall spring rate

Sizes - information usually engraved on the ends or etched into the sides.

Metric: 160-60-110 (tender 40-60-50)
160 - spring open length (mm)
60 - spring internal diameter (mm) 60 or 36
110 - spring rate (N/mm)

Imperial: 5x2.25x500

5 - spring open length (")

2.25 - spring internal diameter (") 2.25 or 1.9

500 - spring (lbs/inch)

Compressive coil springs are most commonly used.

The spring rate is a function or wire dimeter and number of active coils.

Progressive springs have a rate that increases as they are compressed - this varies the number of active coils. As the spring is compressed some of the coils bottom out.

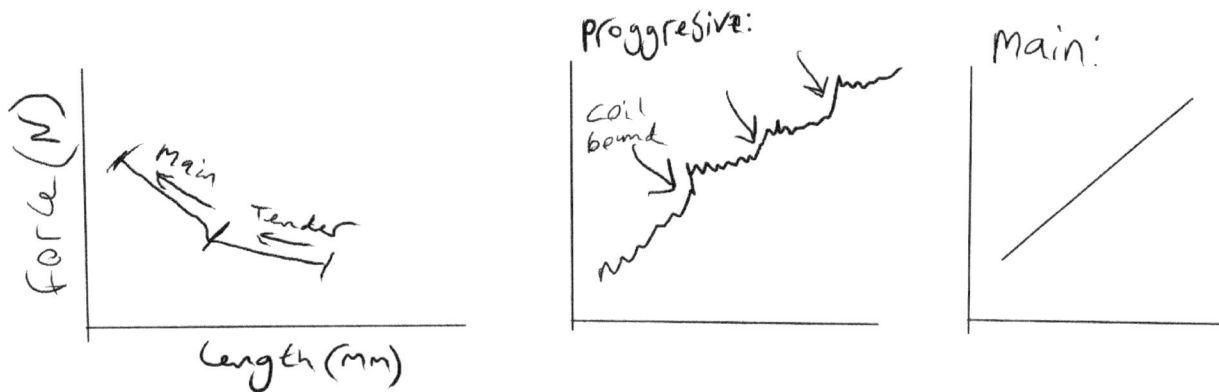

Preload:

Pre-load is a condition where some compression is applied to the spring before it is subject to any additional compressive load from the vehicle. Pre (before) load.

Pre load describes the amount of compression a spring is under in its rest state.

Minimal pre load is often used to hold the coil spring in place at full extension (at the rear commonly).

However pre load can be used as an effective tuning tool (measured in turns of open length)

Loading the spring prior to vertical load:

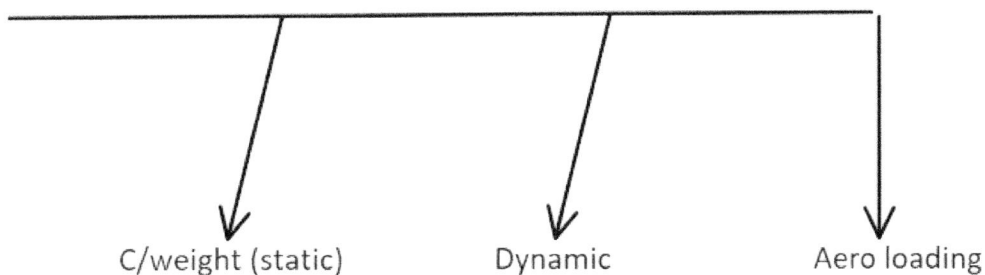

C/weight (static)   Dynamic   Aero loading

Lower spring perch as available ride height adjustment, pre load is not considered.

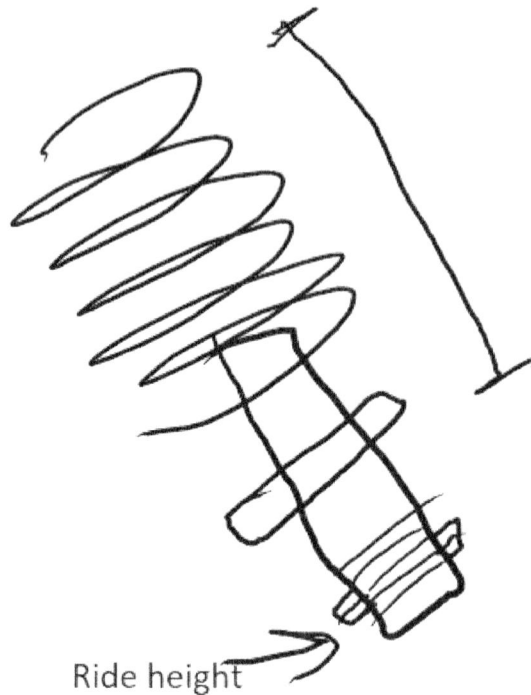

Ride height

A 300 N/mm spring with 450N of pre load has been compressed by 1.5 mm in its rest state.

The spring will not compress further until a force EXCEEDING 450N is applied.

If this were installed on a race car, as the corner is lowered onto the ground there would be no deflection until 450N (around 46kg) of vehicle weight is applied.

Pre load > compression

Naturally it wants to return to its open length rest state.

100 lbs/inch spring

1/2" pre load = 50 lbs - the car must overcome 50lbs of load on that corner before the spring begins to compress.

300N/mm × 1.5mm displacement = 450N pre load

As pre load is initially applied it will have the simple effect of increasing the ride height. This can be compensated for with a pushrod adjustment if required.

Only have pre load on the front due to traction on the rear - Radical PR6

Limits droop travel. Once the load on the spring is less than the pre load, it is effectively at full extension, which prevents the wheel from moving in rebound any further. This can be used to deliberately unload the inside wheel.

If more than one corner weight of the car is applied in pre load the suspension will not move until sufficient aerodynamic load (downforce) is applied to "break" the pre load. This is sometimes referred to a running more than 100% pre load (100% pre load = the weight of the corner of the car).

Droop - wheel travel (extension/rebound) when the car body is lifted.

Running 100% preload or more example:

When the spring preload has not been exceeded the suspension will not move, giving an infinite stiffness. This has the effect of making the car very reactive, with an excellent change of direction.

Benefits of preload found on slow quick changing corners.

The table below represents a race car with a corner weight of 150 kg and that generates 30 kgf per corner at 70 km/h.

Pre load	Force to break preload	Speed to break preload
50%	-75 kgf	0 km/h
100%	0 kgf	0 km/h
120%	+30 kgf	70 km/h

Running more than 100% preload in combination with bump rubbers allows the possibility of running 3 spring stiffness'. This would give excellent change of direction at very low speed, good compliant mechanical grip in the mid speed and increased stiffness at higher speed to support the aero load.

1 - Preload (Low corner speed)

2 - Spring rate (Mid corner speed)

3 - Spring rate and bump rubbers (High corner speed)

Spring Rate Testing:

Intercomp and Longarce are the main suppliers - £1000

Torsion Bars:

Quick to change, not available in anything but linear currently (no progressive). Attracted to rocker arm (aka bell crank). Made from sprung steel.

- In a torsion spring the elastic properties of a twisted bar are used to produce a linear spring rate much like that of a coil spring.
- By altering the diameter of the bar, the corresponding linear spring rate is also changed.
- A larger diameter bar giving a stiffer linear spring rate.
- The main advantages of torsion bar suspension are durability, easy adjustability of ride eight, and it takes up less of the vehicles interior volume compared to coil springs.
- A disadvantage is that unlike coil springs they usually cannot provide a progressive spring rate.

15.0 Car Set Up/Handling Issues

What to know before:

- Current set up of car - tyre spec (compound, set number, slicks, inter, wets), track (green/rubbered in, dry damp wet) & ambient (air temp, wind direction (Silverstone, Snett) conditions)
- What is adjustable and how (castor, camber, toe, correct tools? C-spanner)
- Measuring tools - tyre pressure gauge, tyre temp gauge, ride height measuring tool (tape measure, steel rule, calliper, ride height block), camber gauge & tracking gauges - flat patch

Tyre pressure:

Manufactures will give best hot temp - not doming for example

20-22 psi HOT, for example

HOT - 22 psi

Mechanical understeer - front - 21 psi, rear - 22.5-23 psi

Mechanical oversteer - front - 22.5 psi, rear - 21 psi

Tyre temperature:

- Spread across the tyre - F- 10 - 15c, R - 5 - 10c
- Axle ratios - axle working harder than the other one, compound splits

Toe:

(Assume - no thrust angle)

F: (Driver sensitive)

No bite on initial turn in - more toe out - unstable (steering wheel) - toe in

R: Instability - more toe in

(+/- 4-5mm across the axle)

Lots of stability - more toe out

Damper settings:

Low speed bump:

High speed bump: (Never force the adjusters)

Start stiff then back off

Bumps, undulations, kerbs

Too soft: Bottom

Pitch, roll - combination of.

Too hard:

Which kerbs - needs to know car and circuit? If kerbs are too aggressive - soften

Rebound:

Pitch -

Braking: Rear instability - lack of droop travel, steering sensitive.<Brake bias> Front instability - excess bump travel - front bump increase, rear rebound increase

Accelerating: Understeer - stiffen rear bump (2 clicks) (soften rear rebound (1)), stiffen front rebound (2). Oversteer - soften rear bump, soften front rebound

Patter - generic stiffness - spring of ARB related

Ride Height:

- Made with an aero principle
- Legality (front - rake) - rule book

Rake (made with an aero principle) can be a powerful tuning tool with regards to shifting aero balance, whilst the stability/variance of ride height needs to be appropriately controlled. Adjustments usually based on rear ride height. Adjusted by drop links, pushrods, etc.

- Raise rear ride height (understeer)   Oversteer aero opposite
- Drop front ride height (understeer)

Venturi - centre of pressure forwards

Aero:

Aero - balance - tuning

    - drag vs downforce - condition or track specific (eg Snett 200 - low drag, Brands (Indy) - high DF) Adjustability - wings F+R, dive planes - packages - noses, side pods, rear tubs.

- Driver (aware where the issues are happening eg high speed zones, defies the point)
- Wind direction
- Tyre wear or race progression

Anti-roll bars:

Can change the leverage or thickness (blade - cross section change)

- Non driven axle - stiffer ARB
                - maintain traction for driven axle

Reduction in body roll

" geo change

" independence

Steady state - cornering without change inputs (throttle/brakes)

Shift mechanical grip - stiffer provides less grip, soften provides more grip. Soft gives compliance.

Roll stiffness (per axle) cars stiffness in roll as per a conventional spring rate but in degrees rather than linear displacement. Function of ARB stiffness and its leverage or motion ratio.

Springs & Packers (rubbers)

Springs - are a main tuning item on the car:

- Handling
- Ride quality
- Mechanical grip - aero control too without packers, rubbers and tenders
- Support sprung mass

Natural frequency (Hz) of each axle - driven axle, damping coefficient

Softer will provide more grip
Stiffer will provide less grip

Corner weight check
Geo check

Packers -

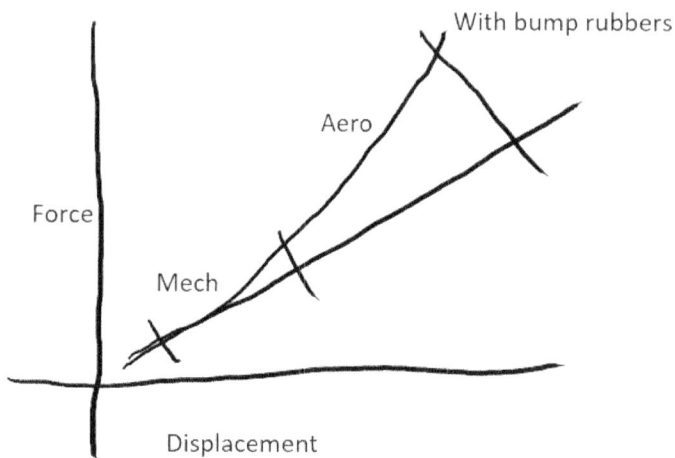

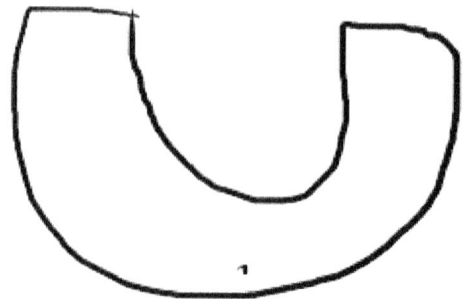

16.0 Steering

Steering:

- Wheel - diameter - small (more feedback, harder to turn)
- Column
- Quick rack
- Bump steer
- Ackerman

Quick rack -

- Ratio - wheel movement vs driver force input
- Rack & pinion
- Electric power assisted steering

Bump Steer:

Bump steer is when the steered wheels steer themselves without input from the steering wheel. Bump in or bump out.

It is caused by bumps in the track interacting with improper length or angle of the suspension and steering linkages, or more specifically, the relationship between the two.

Bump steer should be minimal, it can be adjusted in some systems but not all. Limited adjustment.

For zero bump the tie/track rod must fall between an imaginary line that runs from the upper ball joint through the lower ball joint and an imaginary line that runs through the upper wishbone pivot and the lower wishbone pivot. In additional, the centreline of the tie/track rod must intersect with the instantaneous centre IC created by wishbones.

Basically, the tie rod needed to travel in the same arc as the wishbones. This isn't always so easy in reality as design restrictions and packaging can cause issues. A different in arcs will cause toe in or toe out dependent upon if the arc was bigger or smaller and whether the rack was in front or behind the wheel centreline. Eg, with a rack in front, tie rods too short, the car would toe in under bump.

How much? As little as possible. Knowing how much will help you understand what is going on at least.

Some bump out can be used to assist with corner entry. Bump in is bad.

0.03" (0.762mm) to 0.01" (0.254mm) (per wheel) over the range of useable travel.

Usually if the tie rod line lies below the IC you will have bump in, when above, bump out.

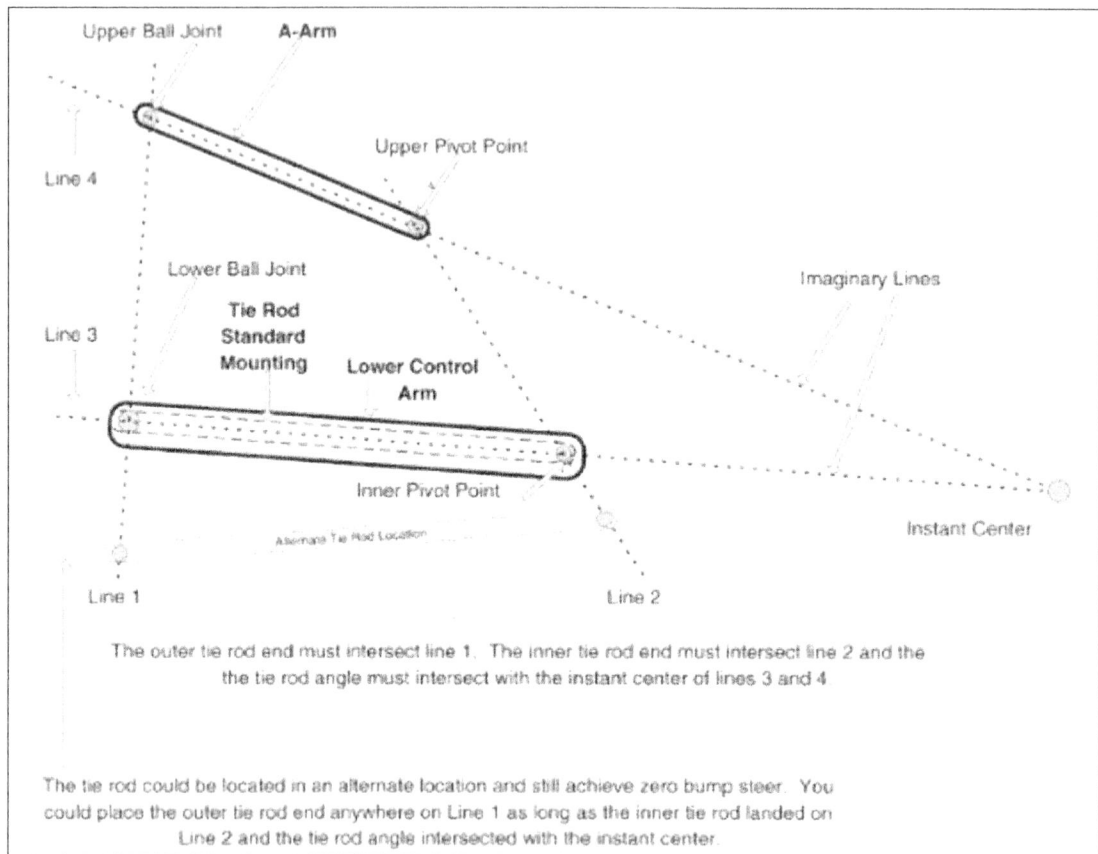

The outer tie rod end must intersect line 1. The inner tie rod end must intersect line 2 and the the tie rod angle must intersect with the instant center of lines 3 and 4

The tie rod could be located in an alternate location and still achieve zero bump steer. You could place the outer tie rod end anywhere on Line 1 as long as the inner tie rod landed on Line 2 and the tie rod angle intersected with the instant center.

Adjustment:

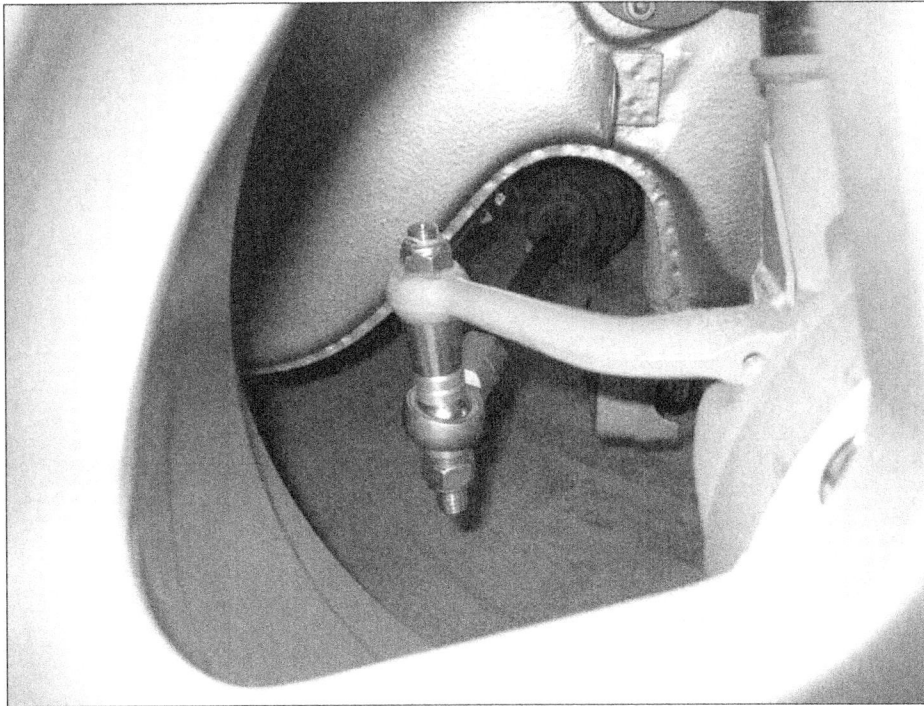

- s/rack up and down
- Outer toe rod joint up and down

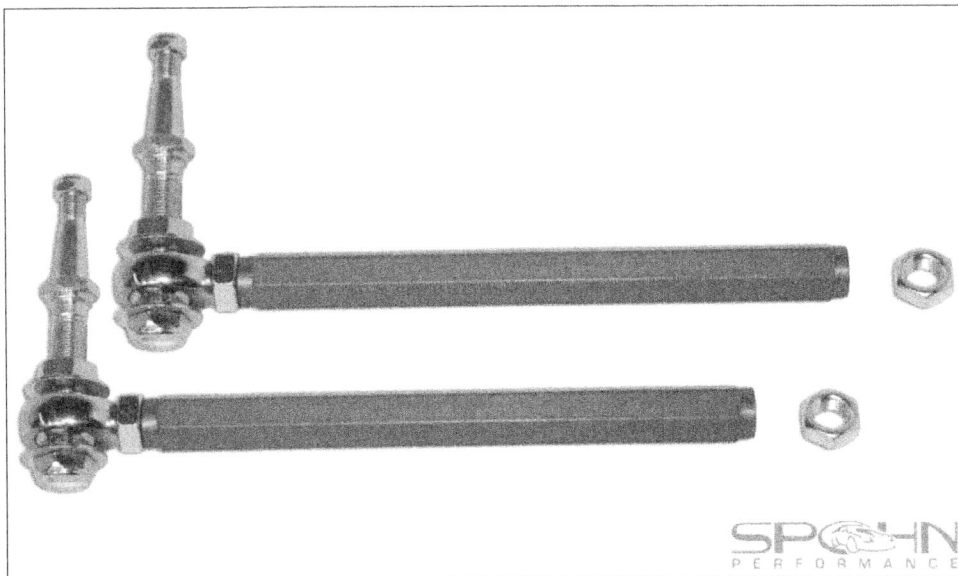

Bump steer gauge

How to -

1. Measure chassis ride height, measure reference on suspension/upright
2. Jack up car and remove wheel and damper. Disconnect ARB.
3. Chock chassis at ride height and support upright at height measured
4. Attach measuring plate to face and lean gauge and DTI is set at 0" ride height and zeroed on dial
5. Jack suspension through range of travel, noting the direction of DTI travel. 1/4" or 1/2" steps. Steer to measure in bump and droop.

Note - steering wheel must be locked in place and hub must not rotate.

17.0 Ackermann

Ackermann angle has three set ups: Pro, anti or true.

Geometry that enables the steering wheels to turn at the correct angle when going around a corner.

Wheels are aligned with the circumference or arc of the circle that the car is travelling.

It is assumed here that the tyres travel around the correct radii which therefore avoid any form of scrub.

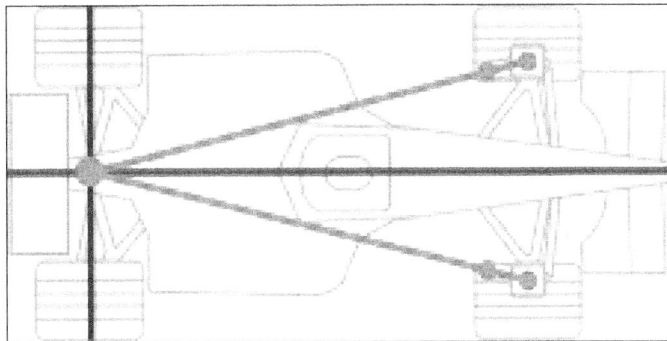

Figure 59 - True Ackermann

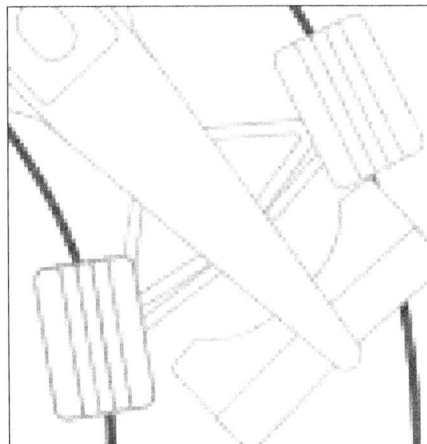

Figure 60 - Cornering with True Ackermann

When the point is directly in the middle of the diff/axle. First pink point is the steering… second is the track rod connecting point.

Pro Ackermann:

Inner turns at a tighter radius to the outer. When compared to the requires radii.

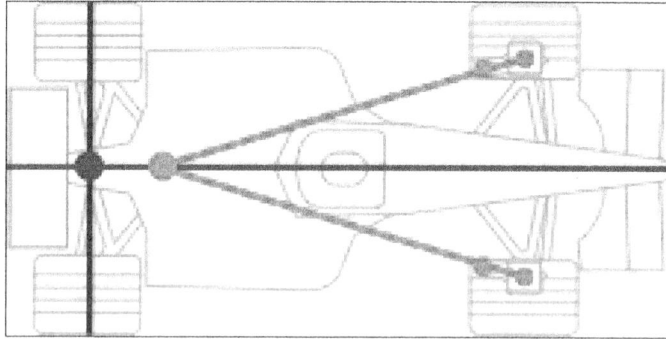

Figure 61 - Pro Ackermann

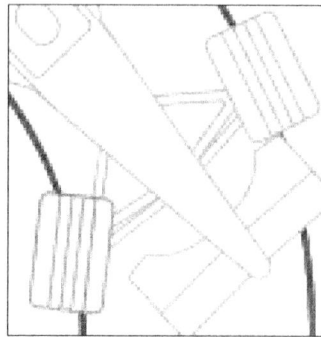

Figure 62 - Cornering with Pro Ackermann

Anti-Ackermann:

Outer turns at a tighter angle then the inside when compared to the required radii.

The inside tyre is generally always carrying less vertical load. Generally speaking, the less vertical load a tyre has, the lower the amount of slip angle it can sustain.

Or more to the point the peak lateral load happens at a lower slip angle, hence the desire to run less steering angle on the inside compared to the outside tyre.

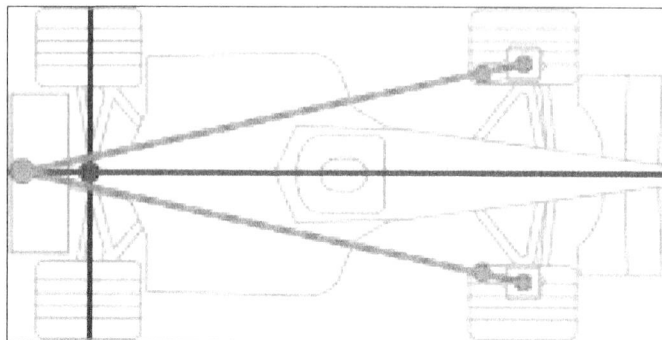

Figure 63 - Anti Ackermann

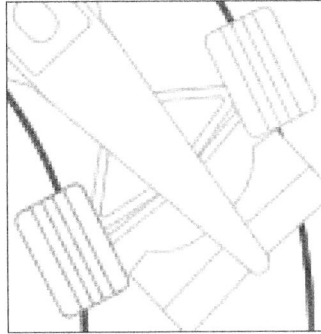

Figure 64 - Cornering with Anti Ackermann

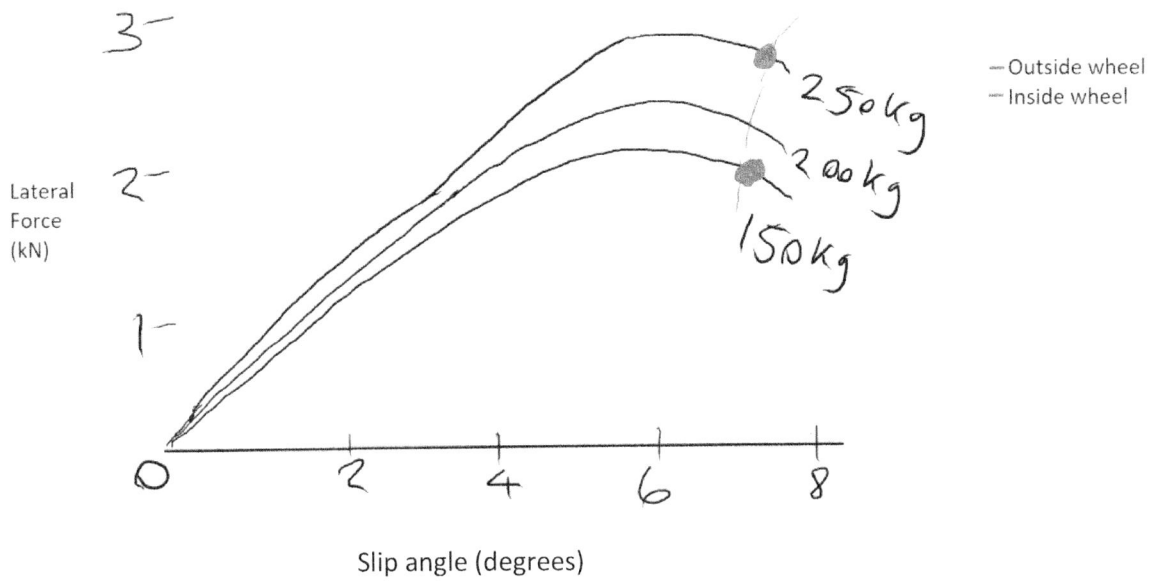

3 —

2 —

Lateral
Force
(kN)

1 —

250kg

200kg

150kg

— Outside wheel
— Inside wheel

O   2   4   6   8

Slip angle (degrees)

You will see that tyre performance is a factor of vertical load and slip angle, with the outer tyre having a higher vertical load than the inner. Slip angle needs to be higher on the outside than the inside. This can be created with Anti-Ackermann.

18.0 Conclusion

This study has researched into suspension designs and layouts on performance vehicles, along with how it affects them in the terms of roll centre control, camber and track change using the software provided. This was including different wishbone and axle layouts, including locations devices, on performance vehicles. Systems including Watts, Panhard, Woblink, Mumford and similar were mentioned. The second section on this study reported on the role of race car dampers. This discussed the types of dampers available, operation, testing methods, the different forms of adjustment and how damping is decided for the given application. Finally, a test on a damper dynamometer was carried out showing the process of the test and analysis of the results from the test.

The second section of the study has shown the dynamics and suspension systems of a single seater performance car. Pre and post set up sheets have been created, along with the evidence of geometry and corner weighting of a single seater performance car. The vehicle was put into the correct set up that was needed that suited the vehicle. An inspection of the vehicle was made in order to show its readiness to race, which was carried out on the vehicle's suspension, steering, tyres and wheels. During this the single seater performance car was analysed to show why it is a competitive racing car. Areas such as the suspension, tyres and steering were examined to shows its effect on stability and handling. The advantages and disadvantages of different types of suspension systems that are on use on many different competition vehicles were discussed.

The third section of the study looked into basics of vehicle dynamics including the sections below:

- Basics
- Wheels and Tyres
- Chassis
- Weight
- Vehicle Adjustment
- Suspension
- Weight Distribution

- Polar Moment of Inertia

- Suspension Development – regarding double wishbone suspension

- Anti-Roll Bars

- King Pin Inclination (KPI)

- Steering Axis Inclination (SAI)

- Scrub Angle

- Rear Suspension

- Motion Ratio and Wheel Rates

- Springs

- Car Set Up and Handling Issues

- Steering

- Ackermann

And many subsections within these topics giving understanding of these topics regarding a vehicle's dynamics.

19.0 References

1. Balancemotorsport.co.uk, (2016). *Suspension Geometry*. [online] Available at: https://balancemotorsport.co.uk/suspension-geometry [Accessed 3 Mar. 2016].

2. Boards.straightdope.com. (2016). *Whats a live rear axle? - Straight Dope Message Board*. [online] Available at: http://boards.straightdope.com/sdmb/showthread.php?t=130114 [Accessed 14 Mar. 2016].

3. Bolles, B. (2008). *Stock Car Dynamics - Racing Suspension Setup - Circle Track Magazine*. [online] Hot Rod. Available at: http://www.hotrod.com/how-to/chassis-suspension/ctrp-0811-suspension-setup/ [Accessed 16 Mar. 2016].

4. Forums.justcommodores.com.au. (2011). *Vp - live axle or IRS*. [online] Available at: http://forums.justcommodores.com.au/vn-vp-holden-commodore-1988-1993/178062-vp-live-axle-irs.html [Accessed 14 Mar. 2016].

5. Homebuiltairplanes.com. (2013). *Landing gear shock absorber deflection - Page 2*. [online] Available at: http://www.homebuiltairplanes.com/forums/aircraft-design-aerodynamics-new-technology/16323-landing-gear-shock-absorber-deflection-2.html [Accessed 14 Mar. 2016].

6. Moog.com. (2016). *Automotive Structural Testing - 4-Poster Test Rig | Moog*. [online] Available at: http://www.moog.com/markets/automotive/automotive-test-simulation/automotive-structural-testing/4-poster-test-rig/ [Accessed 12 Jan. 2016].

7. Roll Center Understood. (2016). [online] Thecartech.com. Available at: http://www.thecartech.com/subjects/auto_eng2/Roll_Center.htm [Accessed 8 Mar. 2016].

8. Penskeshocks.com. (2016). *Penske Shocks*. [online] Available at: http://www.penskeshocks.com/ [Accessed 14 Mar. 2016].

9. Smith, J. (2013). *Smith's Fundamentals of Motorsport Engineering*. Cheltenham: Hillier's, pp.88-91.

10. Spa-uk.co.uk. (2016). *SPA Design: experts in motorsport technology and carbon fibre composite fabrication; supplier of professional racing products and race car accessories*. [online] Available at: http://www.spa-uk.co.uk/dynamometers [Accessed 4 Feb. 2016].

11. Susprog.com. (2016). *Suspension design software SuspTypes*. [online] Available at: http://www.susprog.com/susptype.htm [Accessed 16 Mar. 2016].

12. Timskelton.com. (2016). *panhard bar*. [online] Available at: http://www.timskelton.com/lightning/race_prep/suspension/panhard.htm [Accessed 15 Mar. 2016].

13. Young, B. (2016). *Woblink linkage - Live axle or deDion 3 or 4 trailing links*. [online] Bevenyoung.com.au. Available at: http://www.bevenyoung.com.au/woblink.html [Accessed 16 Mar. 2016].

14. Allon White, (2016). *Wheel Alignment*. [online] Available at: https://allonwhite.co.uk/data/upload/files/Wheel%20Camber.jpg [Accessed 27 Feb. 2016].

15. Balancemotorsport.co.uk, (2016). *Suspension Geometry*. [online] Available at: https://balancemotorsport.co.uk/suspension-geometry [Accessed 3 Mar. 2016].

16. Core77, (2016). *Going Dutch*. [online] Available at: http://www.core77.com/posts/6070/Going-Dutch [Accessed 29 Feb. 2016].

17. Double Wishbone Suspension - Explained. (2012). [online] YouTube. Available at: https://www.youtube.com/watch?v=DsEmK1M87VQ [Accessed 4 Mar. 2016].

18. Ferrari F2012. (2012). [online] Gforcef1.files.wordpress.com. Available at: https://gforcef1.files.wordpress.com/2012/02/7429269.jpg [Accessed 4 Mar. 2016].

19. F1technical.net, (2016). [online] Available at: http://www.f1technical.net/f1db/cars/images/1968/honda-ra302-drawing.gif [Accessed 27 Feb. 2016].

20. How Car Suspensions Work. (2005). [online] HowStuffWorks. Available at: http://auto.howstuffworks.com/car-suspension4.htm [Accessed 4 Mar. 2016].

21. Leakylugnut.com, (2016). [online] Available at: http://leakylugnut.com/wp-content/uploads/2013/01/toe1.jpg [Accessed 27 Feb. 2016].

22. MacPherson Strut - Explained. (2012). [online] YouTube. Available at: https://www.youtube.com/watch?v=1fvJMxErfms [Accessed 4 Mar. 2016].

23. Pushrod Suspension - Explained. (2012). [online] I.ytimg.com. Available at: https://i.ytimg.com/vi/zwYybcpBeZI/hqdefault.jpg [Accessed 4 Mar. 2016].

24. Pushrod Suspension - Explained. (2012). [online] YouTube. Available at: https://www.youtube.com/watch?v=zwYybcpBeZI [Accessed 4 Mar. 2016].

25. Smith, J. (2013). *Smith's Fundamentals of Motorsport Engineering*. Cheltenham: Hillier's, p.209.

26. Smith, J. (2013). *Smith's Fundamentals of Motorsport Engineering*. Cheltenham: Hillier's, pp.94-100.

27. Startline.org.uk, (2016). *StartlineOnLine*. [online] Available at: http://www.startline.org.uk/slol65/Tyres/tyres.htm [Accessed 2 Mar. 2016].

28. Tamiya. (2016). [online] Tamiya.com. Available at: http://www.tamiya.com/english/products/58288ferrari_f2001/photo7.jpg [Accessed 4 Mar. 2016].

29. Tirerack.com, (2016). [online] Available at: http://www.tirerack.com/images/tires/tiretech/diag_thrust.gif [Accessed 26 Feb. 2016].

30. Unique Cars and Parts. (2016). [online] Uniquecarsandparts.com.au. Available at: http://www.uniquecarsandparts.com.au/images/how_to_repair/Suspension/Suspension_2.jpg [Accessed 4 Mar. 2016].

31. Vikingspeedshop.com, (2016). [online] Available at: http://www.vikingspeedshop.com/wp-content/uploads/caster.jpg [Accessed 26 Feb. 2016].

Printed in Great Britain
by Amazon